Praise for Education's Ecosystems

"A remarkable narrative, weaving the practical science with the lived experience of learning science, taking the ecology idea from science and showing its all important application to education. A must read for all science educators and those with interest in learning in any area. . . . Through example, stories, and imagined dialogues, the perspective of the education ecosystem is brought to life. A treatise of education as much as a set of thought provoking chapters that will stimulate thought about current learning practice." — **Caroline Haythornthwaite**, Syracuse University

"Bertram Bruce calls the kinds of learning he describes 'experiential learning because it involves learning through experiencing life.' And, of course, this is true. I know of no other scholar or colleague who so remarkably makes me think deeply about both learning and teaching. So, as I read, I thought predictably perhaps of my own learning and what resonated most with me over the years. Strangely enough, my most satisfying learning happened in a ninth grade New York Latin class in which I seemed to oddly excel and, as a result, fell in love with languages. My study of Latin, for which I won a New York Classical Club award, provoked my immersion in the field of linguistics with IndoEuropean leading to Proto-Germanic and a love of the modern day Germanic languages. Living in Germany for some years after my Latin class, and experiencing daily learning in a Germanic culture also contributed meaningfully to my love of dialects and here again Bertram Bruce's embrace of experience coupled with learning comes into play. School experience contributed meaningfully when, back in the states, the study of historical linguistics, and my fascination with phonological change, undergirded my life in English Departments (my love of Middle English and its relation to Middle French, for example) and a quick study of Frisian, a fascinating language most closely related to English and its Germanic heritage. All of this is to say, that *Education's Ecosystems: Learning through Life* led me to think about the explosive aspect of my school learning experiences—which fostered new learning experiences that enhanced my life. As he says so well, 'Learning [is] a living process . . . in which each experience [leads] to learning and in turn to new experiences. When learning is separated from life, it becomes sterile.' Indeed." —**Gail E. Hawisher**, University of Illinois

"At a moment when the need for new ways of thinking about the connections between learning and nature is literally overheating, this book is an invitation to engage more wisely, more imaginatively, and more ethically. Here, we are invited to feel what it is to be immersed in an ecosystem, enticed to experience relations-in-the-wild between Whitehead, *sofrito*, Gandhi, discarded computers, fungi, Freinet, niches, Nepalize courtyards, and frogs. The principles that Bruce taps for an Ecosystems Learning Framework are not merely an analytic model; rather, they are refreshing springs of cool ways of knowing, destined to grow something beautiful and fertile." —**Kevin Leander**, Vanderbilt University

"This book will get you excited about learning again. Through stories about busy lichen, an unscented skunk, a decapitated frog, a museum-school in Fort Worth, a library-park in Medellín, a Nepalese courtyard, a Gandhian worldview, a dancing hologram, and an imagined dialogue among three Greek goddesses, Bertram Bruce lays out a theoretical model called the Ecosystems Learning Framework (ELF). The ecosystem(s) approach provides both a starting point for learning and a metaphor about how we meaningfully learn and why. Formal schooling still matters, but this book shows how life *itself* is the curriculum, and by embracing life in its fully connected, embedded, embodied, adaptive and emergent ways, we can see exciting new pathways for both learning and participating in a healthy, flourishing, morally sustainable democracy." —**Maureen Hogan**, Education, University of Alaska at Fairbanks

"This book bravely proposes the theoretical and practical foundations of 'Learning through Life.' It guides the reader through an enthralling learning experience full of a diverse set of personal, historical, and philosophical examples on the concept of Education Ecosystems." —**Iván M. Jorrín Abellán**, Professor of Education, Kennesaw State University

"Addressing learning in ecosystems in its full and vibrant sense—cognitive, social, sensory—Bruce invites us to grapple with important questions, re-imagining the purposes and possibilities of education. Intensifying connections between the formal and informal settings and across diverse cultural contexts, time periods, disciplines, and types of learning, this is a wonderfully engaging and inviting contribution. A compelling read!" —**Liora Bresler**, Professor, College of Education, University of Illinois

"Bertram Bruce's new book makes a just-in-time contribution to understanding the massive shift in educational paradigms through which we are living.

Connecting pedagogical principles to ecological models, critical democratic theory, and pragmatic philosophy, Bruce has concocted a rich elixir for the future of education. His work shines a light on new and positive directions for formal schooling through the integration of informal learning, community participation, and digital tools." —**Judith Davidson**, Professor, College of Education, University of Massachusetts Lowell

"Bruce's highly readable book is an important reminder that education, if it is to be connected to lived experience, takes place in an ecosystem of interconnected venues from the home to the classroom to the museum to the natural environment. When used wisely this ecosystem can reshape learning in ways that are consistent with the best of progressive education." —**Walter Feinberg**, Philosophy of Education, University of Illinois

Education's Ecosystems

Education's Ecosystems

Learning through Life

Bertram C. Bruce

ROWMAN & LITTLEFIELD
Lanham • Boulder • New York • London

Published by Rowman & Littlefield
An imprint of The Rowman & Littlefield Publishing Group, Inc.
4501 Forbes Boulevard, Suite 200, Lanham, Maryland 20706
www.rowman.com

6 Tinworth Street, London SE11 5AL, United Kingdom

Copyright © 2020 by Bertram C. Bruce

Some of the text in chapter 3 is adapted from "Coffee Cups, Frogs, and Lived Experience," in *International Journal of Progressive Education* 4, no. 2 (2008): 22–39.

Portions of chapters 10–12 were drawn from "Community as Curriculum: Nurturing the Ecosystem of Education," *Schools* 15, no. 1 (2018): 122–39.

All rights reserved. No part of this book may be reproduced in any form or by any electronic or mechanical means, including information storage and retrieval systems, without written permission from the publisher, except by a reviewer who may quote passages in a review.

British Library Cataloguing in Publication Information Available

Library of Congress Control Number: 2020932590

ISBN 978-1-4758-5119-9 (cloth)
ISBN 978-1-4758-5120-5 (pbk.)
ISBN 978-1-4758-5121-2 (electronic)

For my wife, Susan, in appreciation for her intellectual, emotional, and practical support throughout life, including the writing of this book.

Contents

Foreword	xiii
Preface	xvii
Acknowledgments	xxi
Introduction	xxiii
1 Ecosystems Learning Framework	1
2 The Whole Frog	13
3 Why Do We Educate?	23
4 Diversity in Ways to Learn	41
5 Networking	57
6 Emergent Properties	67
7 Finding and Constructing Learning Niches	83
8 Interpretation of Learning Spaces	101
9 A Dialogue on Formal and Informal Learning	117
10 The Ecosystem Curriculum	129
Conclusion	153
Bibliographic Note	159
Index	161
About the Author	165

Foreword

As a progressive educator specializing in experiential teaching and learning, I have spent the last few decades exploring ways to contextualize learning environments. Early in my career as a science educator, I helped found the Progressive Education Network, dedicated to promoting the development of individuals as active learners within a school community and as engaged citizens in the broader world. To this end, my work explores ways to engage students in learning through meaningful, authentic projects within students' neighborhoods. This work led to several collaborations with Bertram Bruce, known to most people as Chip. In 2013 we edited a special edition for the *International Journal of Progressive Education*, and in 2016 Chip invited me to edit a section of the *International Handbook of Progressive Education*.

In over twenty years of educational research, I recognize that people learn in a variety of ways. In this vein, Chip has written a text that takes seriously the idea of ecosystems as used in biology to characterize learning. The learning ecosystems metaphor means that we learn in the classroom and online or in apprenticeship as well as formal spaces. In *Education's Ecosystems* Chip introduces an Ecosystems Learning Framework (ELF) that cultivates integrative learning across a variety of modalities. The ELF view of life and learning consists of five key characteristics (diversity in ways to learn, networking, emergent properties, finding and constructing learning niches, and interpretation of learning ecosystems).

The ELF describes diversity in types of learning in an expansive way and examines interaction among emergent properties, creativity, and interpretation, thereby going beyond the usual presentation. There are diverse examples across nations, time periods, disciplines, and types of learning. The ecosystem theme provides coherence without erasing the differences across situations and helps to provide an understanding of why and how different learning situations serve learners in different ways.

Ecosystem education accentuates the interdependence between formal and informal learning environments, which can be exploited in curricula, the design of learning materials, and approaches to foster learning. Informal learning is often mistakenly considered an alternative to, as opposed to complementary with, formal instruction and is mostly associated with learning outside of school. The last fifteen years of research by neuroscientists and psychologists about how people learn reinforces the way learning is organized and supported in informal environments, which are a large part of the educational ecosystem. In contemporary education, citizen science projects often engage students with learning in and about the community by combining formal with informal learning.

In my own work, an example of this was the invasive lionfish project, which explored the impacts of invasive species. Local fisheries provide lionfish to university researchers who work with high school teachers and their students. During the project, students dissect lionfish, collect stomach contents, and perform DNA analysis and barcoding to identify lionfish prey. Students interviewed stated feeling like scientists contributing to real science. The connections to community resources made learning for the students more relevant, challenging, and memorable.

This book is valuable for educators teaching in a holistic way or preparing teachers to view learning as an accumulation of experiences, by providing a theoretical foundation for engaging and relevant learning that occurs in schools, community centers, libraries, museums, zoos, science centers, or informal clubs. The Great Smokey Mountains Institute at Tremont provides a good example of a holistic approach to learning that combines formal and informal learning. Tremont developed a cooperative teaching model for formal K–12 teachers to team up with Tremont naturalists during a teacher escape weekend to connect subjects and standards, practice experiential teaching methods, and develop confidence with outdoor learning. Tremont's cooperative teaching model embodies all five key characteristics of ELF.

After an initial career as an environmental scientist, I appreciate how Chip connects the formal and informal learning environments with the ecosystem metaphor. My colleague, Mike Dias, and I have been researching experiential learning of thru-hikers on the Appalachian Trail. The ELF provides a lens through which to view our research. The thru-hikers we interviewed learned in diverse ways drawing on their formal knowledge, Internet resources and applications, guidebooks, and social interactions with fellow thru-hikers, friends, and family. Their learning network bridged previous formal knowledge with new knowledge from the nature trail experience and promoted social construction of ideas with the people with whom they interacted. New thoughts and understandings about science encompassing nature, organisms, and biological functions emerged from the experience. Along their journey, thru-hikers constructed and reconstructed their learning as they experienced nature and interacted with others. Thus, each thru-hiker individually interpreted their learning ecosystem to make sense of their experiences.

Education's Ecosystems illustrates that learning does not occur in a vacuum. The diverse ecosystems that humans inhabit provide for a different lived experience for everyone. Some environmental conditions provide substantial variations to learning conditions while other differences are more subtle. Diverse ecosystems both positively and negatively influence learning context and certainly impact individual understandings and learning. Some ecosystems offer limited opportunities for learning or conditions that actively hinder learning like hunger, poverty, social stress, drugs, and pollution. The ecosystems approach provides ways to intervene, to yield more beneficial learning for all students and the possibility for rendering productive learning in negative ecosystems. This book offers a radical rethinking of how education is defined and organized.

John L. Pecore, PhD
Associate Professor and Askew Institute Research Fellow
Associate Chair, Department of Teacher Education
and Educational Leadership
University of West Florida

Preface

Frisky and Blossom are long gone now. In any case, I wouldn't recognize them if they showed up today, but they were among my best early teachers. They were descented skunks. I met them when my mother enrolled me, as a three-year-old, in the Frisky and Blossom Club held at what was then the Fort Worth Children's Museum. That club was the first class of the Museum School, now one of the largest such programs in the world, having served over 212,000 children. But starting in the summer of 1950, the club had only five members, counting myself.

The club operated several days a week out of an old house. There were outdoor benches where we met for activities. We played with Frisky and Blossom, learned about rocks and fossils, and learned through other artifacts the museum provided. We also talked about things we liked to do. The kind couple who ran the program helped us connect those interests to each other's and to the larger world of nature.

MUSEUM SCHOOL

Later, I took other classes at the growing Museum School. These included insects, rocks and fossils, and astronomy. I joined the Astronomy Club, and I still have my loose-leaf notebook from experiences there. It includes issues of *Sky & Telescope* from 1956, diagrams of constellations, and notes from our classes. It also describes our field trips, in which we sat on a hillside watching for meteors or studying the Milky Way (a stupendous sight available to anyone on Earth to see in the days before light pollution).

I also participated in a program to spot enemy aircraft, presumably Russian bombers that had somehow missed being seen on their way to Fort Worth. I don't know whether I helped save the nation, but I remember being excited about a chance to contribute and learning how to identify planes by their sound and silhouette. I still have a book of astronomy, which I won for spotting planes.

Although my writing in that notebook seems rudimentary compared to that of the nine- and ten-year-olds I see today, it recalls for me the joy I felt in expanding my imagination. I listed distances of planets not because I was to be tested on it or because it was good preparation for middle school but because the museum classes had awakened my senses. They concocted a living organism out of the natural curiosity of a child, knowledgeable and caring adults, interesting books, charts, and images, and the clear Texas skies.

What emerged from the Astronomy Club can be said about the other activities as well. I remember searching for insects in the botanical gardens and making boxes for mounting them. I can still identify insects by their order and was interested to read about the renaissance of the order, Notoptera (commonly called "gladiators"). In fact, a characteristic of all the experiences I had at the Museum School is that they didn't stop when the class or club ended. Instead of covering a topic and moving on, the Museum School caused me to open up, to seek to extend and enhance those experiences.

Another characteristic of these experiences was that they were never captured by their title—"rocks and fossils" or "insects." The goal was not to "master" the material in some circumscribed area. Through the insects class, I learned about cigar boxes (to hold the mounted insects), carbon tetrachloride (now banned as unsafe!), painting and homasote, the Greek language, flowers in the botanical gardens, diseases, history, and much more.

Through "rocks and fossils" I learned about plaster of Paris, two-dimensional and three-dimensional representations, dinosaurs, evolution, geology, oil exploration, and the age of the Earth. In contrast to some of the formal instruction I was then receiving in school, this was a living process, a statistically unpredictable one, in which each experience led to learning and in turn to new experiences.

WHAT IT MEANT TO ME

It is impossible to identify all the ways the Museum School affected me. Does it include that I later married Susan, who was working at the Boston Children's Museum? Its many tendrils included reading a biography of Roy Chapman Andrews as a teenager and fantasizing about exploring the world; loving canoeing and hiking to this day; choosing to major in biology in college; being a regular reader of *Scientific American*, *Natural History*, *Smithsonian*, and *National Geographic*; participating in Science for the People; engaging in citizen science projects; and wanting to share a love of science with my children.

The most pervasive effect for me is how it has shaped the way I think about learning and life. I began to see these activities as participation in an ecosystem. Arising in the 1930s, the ecosystem concept breathed depth and breadth into ecological studies by emphasizing the tight relationships among both living and nonliving parts of a natural system. The system could develop, transform, and sustain itself through the emergent properties of these interacting components and through exchanges with other systems near and far. This is the kernel of the educational concept to be fleshed out here.

The learning ecosystem for me included different venues, such as the Museum School, the hillside to view meteors, and the people I shared it with. Learning developed as a consequence of that participation and in turn enabled deeper participation in future experiences. Only later did I come to appreciate the privilege these opportunities gave me.

Not surprisingly, I first experienced school as an interruption, even a negation of that learning through life ("Sit down and finish your workbooks!"; "That doesn't belong in the classroom!"; "What were you doing instead of your homework?"). The testing mania of today only exacerbates that tendency.

When learning is separated from life, it becomes sterile: How many hours did all of us spend doing calculations in math classes, and how many of us feel confident in math, care about it, spend time thinking about it? If that approach helped people develop a lifelong passion for learning, critical social engagement, and caring for others, I'd reconsider my views about it, but all too often those qualities emerge in spite of formal instruction. I've too often encountered people who say they "don't do science," "don't like to read," "know nothing about art," or "can't deal with figures." They emerge from schooling having acquired few practical skills and feeling relief that they don't have to study anymore.

The Museum School taught me a lot about the world. To this day, I can tell you the difference between *Diplodocus*, Diptera, and dipper. I'm probably less wary of skunks than I should be. But, more importantly, it taught me that the process of learning and growing is both challenging and energizing. The energizing aspect comes because the learning is connected to things the child cares about. That caring in turn is what makes it possible for the child to invest deeply in what would otherwise be daunting tasks. In the end, the learning becomes deeply embedded. The joy of learning comes from expanding the imagination.

My experiences with Frisky and Blossom taught me about the value of connecting to ideas that matter and of being deeply engaged in life. They showed me that joy in one's experiences is the best source for lifelong learning. Over time, I came to see that "wholehearted, purposeful activity proceeding in a social environment" was not just the best but in fact the only way that we really learn. Influenced no doubt by Frisky and Blossom, I saw that thriving as a living organism and learning in a connected way were essentially alternate descriptions of the same process.

As an educator, I now describe the kind of learning I just described as experiential learning because it involves learning through experiencing life. A topic like a skunk, an insect, or a planet is part of a system of related things, or in the case of living organisms, an ecosystem. I am part of those ecosystems, and my learning is part of an educational ecosystem. These ecosystems are being transformed by information and communication technologies, changes in the way we live and work, and evolving cultures; learning must change in response.

NEW QUESTIONS

My experiences at the Museum School also raised many questions, which I examine in this book: What is the ecosystem for learning in a globalized world, with social interaction increasingly through electronic media, augmented reality, and technologies that radically extend our senses? Can we extend the kinds of early learning opportunities that I had to others, especially in a world of growing inequality? How does situated, grounded learning relate to learning about others across cultures and time periods? Where does formal education fit into this picture?

If experiential learning is so powerful, can it realize larger educational goals, such as developing engaged citizens, fostering moral development, learning about life beyond the immediate environment, or nurturing participation in social and economic life? The Museum School itself meant more than just play in the neighborhood. What is education's ecosystem in a world radically changed since 1950?

Acknowledgments

The ideas presented here, the projects, and the experiences derive any value they may have from my interactions with a large number of generous and creative colleagues. It is a good example of emergence as discussed in the ecosystem model. The ideas reflect criticism, assistance, and guidance from many people, making it much better than it would have been had I been writing in a solitary garret.

For comments on the ideas presented here and the manuscript per se, and obviously absolving them of its flaws, I'd like to thank Liora Bresler, Leo Casey, Phil Crowley, Judith Davidson, Walter Feinberg, Mike Fisher, Gail Hawisher, Caroline Haythornthwaite, Maureen Hogan, Shihkuan Hsu, José Emiliano Ibáñez, Sharon Irish, Iván M. Jorrín, Kshitiz Khanal, Kevin Leander, Karen MacQueen, Robbie McClintock, Chaebong Nam, John Pecore, Erika Pfammatter, Taffy Raphael, Kamana Regmi, Fátima Cruz Souza, Gerry Stahl, Marc Strauss, Sabhyata Timsina, and Luz Zambrano.

My editor, Tom Koerner, provided useful guidance on a number of points. He also suggested the main title, which proved to fit the message of the book quite well.

I cannot thank my family (Susan, Emily, and Stephen) enough for their support throughout this process, including making time available and providing encouragement, but also extremely helpful discussions and critique of the text.

Introduction

> Our current learning culture is stale and reeking of industrialism. We educate children like they are blank slates and passive vessels. We pry out their talents and gifts until there are none left. And we cage them up like livestock for at least twelve years of their lives. And then we throw them into the scary and uncomfortable world of the unknown.
>
> —Nikhil Goyal[1]

The reader of this book is anyone interested in democratic education. This means here education that enables a democratic society in which every individual has a say and that thrives by supporting the full development of each individual. That sort of education must itself be democratic, respecting the diversity of learners, encouraging meaningful participation, and promoting equality for all.

The ecosystems perspective presented here offers a new way of thinking about how learning through life—work, play, home, family, and community—relates to formal education and its many informal counterparts in libraries, clubs, churches, online, etc. It conceives education broadly as the central process of democratic life. For the educator in formal or informal settings, it provides a theoretical framework for what the best educators are already doing. For the researcher or evaluator, it offers tools for analysis. For anyone it suggests ways to reflect on our own learning through life.

DEMOCRACY AND DEMOCRATIC EDUCATION

Democracy requires citizens with a critical, socially engaged intelligence. That cannot develop through passive learning or indoctrination but through learning opportunities that are complex, challenging, active, collaborative, and meaningful. Thus, democracy implies democratic education. Conversely, democratic education fosters the development of citizens who can participate fully in civic life, not as recipients of a completed system, but as continual creators of it.

Some nations may be judged as farther along the spectrum of both democracy and democratic education than others. But none can be deemed as having fully achieved these aims. Both education and democracy require continual re-creation to meet the new challenges for each generation.

If we consider the United States, we see a nation with some progress toward these goals, but a long way to go. Residential segregation between cities is getting worse. Black children are more likely to grow up in poor neighborhoods than they were fifty years ago.[2] Schooling in general seems to do poorly with issues such as climate change or divides along lines of language, nationality, gender, and religion. It exacerbates income disparities, with the most important indicator of educational success being household income, not hard work by students or dedication of teachers.

Throughout the world today, the pre–World War II song "A Nightingale Sang in Berkeley Square" seems disturbingly a propos, especially the part about the poor puzzled moon looking down with a frown and the world seeming upside down. As of this writing, Greenland is melting, and the Amazon is burning; racism and nationalism are ascendant; the gap between rich and poor is growing; sexual abuse is practiced and praised by world leaders; mass murderers easily obtain weapons of mass destruction and turn toxic rhetoric into reality; and there is unaccountable hunger and untreated disease. These problems do not occur in isolation, but are connected through a system of historical, economic, and cultural relations.

Are these, and too many other disasters, the consequence of what we have taught to succeeding generations, the ultimate outcome of our devotion to education? Are we even thinking about education in ways that would lead to more productive, equitable, healthy, happy lives for all?

LEARNING ECOSYSTEMS

The metaphor of *learning ecosystem* has achieved prominence for many reasons, among them:

- We now learn in face-to-face settings, online, and in blended and hybrid environments.
- Resources for learning still include textbooks, but also social media, mobile platforms, video, virtual and augmented reality, remote sensors, and a zoo of other new technologies.
- Within an organization, workers learn through formal training, from managers and co-workers, through the Internet, and from family and friends.

In schools, this implies learning from fellow students and friends as well as teachers.

Learning ecosystems described in this way are invariably positive. People need to create, or to recognize, a rich ecosystem. The learners to need to navigate it well to maximize their learning. Only rarely do proponents acknowledge that an ecosystem can be destructive. They can create or reproduce failure. A simple example is that poverty can be a salient aspect of a learning ecosystem, affecting other components, such as school quality or enrichment opportunities.

We need to be aware of the many ways that the ecosystem can shape learning. People involved in corporate training or in universities often tout the positive aspects of their learning ecosystems, such as the user-friendly technologies, the ample multimedia resources, the diverse learning spaces. But it can be equally valuable to consider all the aspects of the ecosystem, even those that just emerged in an unplanned way. Think, for example, of how the centrality of football in the United States shapes the college learning experience for many, not only the players themselves.

This book adopts the ecosystems metaphor, but extends it, seeing diversity in ways to learn in an expansive way. It also considers less cited justifications for a learning ecosystem perspective, such as:

- We now learn across multiple information and community technology–enabled physical and virtual spaces, including three-dimensional virtual worlds.[3]
- Learning is not just a mental process, but a bodily one, involving all the senses—taste, smell, feel, sound, kinesthetics, and more.
- Our muscles, organs, even biome can be said to learn.
- We learn through images, objects, scenes, and the tools we use to explore and manipulate those.
- Learning is a creative process, in which the learner actively constructs the ecosystem. For example, we create or change objects in the environment as one way of enacting learning.
- The learner is an artist, creating and appreciating the world through an aesthetic lens.
- Learning occurs through interactions with nature, including living plants and animals, oceans and prairies, and the moon and stars, as well as through the disembodied media of the text or the Internet.
- The elements of a learning ecosystem are not simply different means to achieve the same learning objective, but part of a complex, interacting system with emergent properties. This means that what is learned may not correspond at all to what was intended to be taught.

- The larger culture in which learning occurs can be more significant than any specific learning activity.
- A consequence of the above is that the learning ecosystem is not always a positive influence; any element, or the ecosystem as a whole, can hinder learning or bend it toward dysfunctional learning.

The learning system perspective provides an alternative to the usual discourse about schooling as the center of education and informal learning as an interesting but less central activity. It conceives learning as occurring in multiple, interconnected spaces. The many components of the system and, more importantly, the connections among those components are the arena in which learning does or does not occur. This provides a different starting point for thinking about education. From this perspective, schools still matter, but they are only part of the story.

STORIES ABOUT THE ECOSYSTEMS OF LEARNING

We now know that trees grow in the context of other trees, fungi, and insects. What is the corresponding ecosystem for human learners? How does an ecosystem for human learning connect with the larger natural ecosystems? How is it evolving? How does it break down, or, in contrast, how does it promote healthy living and learning? What can we do to preserve and strengthen that system? How can we connect formal learning to learning throughout life?

A central concept for any ecosystem is that organisms interact; they participate in and through other organisms, and inorganic structures and materials. In a similar way, humans need successful participation with the natural world and with other people. They can learn and thrive through that participation. Their learning enables fuller participation, and even transformation of that ecosystem.

The core of the book is essentially a set of stories about learning ecosystems. The examples involve both formal and informal learning, but also, crucially, how those activities occur in an ecological relationship. In following these stories, we set aside for the moment the fact that some experiential learning can be valuable without any explicit connection to formal curricula and that some formal, decontextualized learning activities can be useful. Our concern is for the reciprocity.

There are varied examples of the ecosystems perspective across nations, time periods, disciplines, and types of learning. The complexity that comes from wide application of the perspective helps us to understand its full implications and its broad applicability. As in an ecosystem, there is no linear path. Instead, the reader is invited to take a journey through varied realms.

Stepping into each realm can open up new ways of thinking about the purpose and means of education. The goal is to provide a basis for reimagining what education can and should be in the modern world.

No one story should be taken as a model for how to fix education. If anything, they argue against the idea of a simple method or prescription for the ills of education. However, each shows how the ever present connections between formal and informal learning can be enhanced, leading to more fulfilling formal education and a richer life. Beyond that, they should lead us to ask questions about the entire educational enterprise and reinvigorate its role in society.

Our own health depends on connectedness among the organs of our body, with our biome, and in our relations with others. Break those connections and we find that the body suffers, if not dies. Each of the stories here has a similar message. The connections across modes and venues for learning are vital to learning, at the very least enhancing it and more generally providing a way to address the larger educational problems discussed above.

The stories have titles, but those are really just the starting points. One may be about interaction with nature, but then lead to using new information technologies, and from there segue into community action. It is in the nature of the best ecosystem-based learning to be integrative and generative. As an integrative approach, it connects across domains ordinarily considered separate, such as formal/informal, science/art, or academic/vocational. As a generative process, it continually re-creates and expands itself, without a priori restrictions on where the inquiry may lead.

ORGANIZATION OF THE BOOK

If we are to understand how people learn, we need to consider the complete environment for learning. This means looking at work and play, online and offline interactions, formal and informal settings, times together and times alone. It also means considering what happens in school, not starting with that, but at the same time not ignoring it or its unique position in the learning ecosystem.

The book begins with a wide-angle perspective, starting in chapter 1 with the Ecosystems Learning Framework (ELF). The perspective here is that all learning occurs in an ecosystem, including both intentional components and accidental ones. Some of these derive from the surrounding society, such as the nature of the economy.

Chapter 2 asks us to consider the whole frog, emphasizing the importance of connections, and extends to explore new ideas about ecosystems.

Chapter 3 asks, "Why do we educate?" That leads to consideration of various ideas about the aims of education for the individual and for society.

Theories that most shape current educational policy and practice fail to account for both the benefits and the hazards of education ecosystems.

The book continues in chapters 4–8 with stories about how ecosystem-based learning arises and why it matters. These stories reveal learning by means of participation in daily life, through work, and with nature. They also show how learning makes fuller participation possible.

The stories consider communication, through reading, with others nearby, and with news media. They move from learning about the world to changing it, to building or sustaining community and the natural environment that sustains human life. In all of these, both individual integrity and community are imagined and shaped through shared activity.[4] In each case, we see how formal learning can be enriched and extended by connecting it with real-world experience.

Each chapter exhibits all five of the foundational ideas for education ecosystems: *diversity in ways to learn*, *networking*, *emergent properties*, *finding and constructing learning niches*, and *interpretation of learning spaces*. However, the chapters in sequence each emphasize one of the five ideas.

Chapter 9 focuses on education's ecosystems per se, through a dialogue between a defender of decontextualized, formalized learning (Athena) and a proponent of experiential learning (Artemis). Chapter 10 presents an ecosystems curriculum. Although the ELF is a neutral, analytical tool, it can be applied to provide guidelines for making education take better advantage of its ecosystem. The conclusion ends with democratic education, how ecosystem-based pedagogy relates to the existing educational system, and where to go next.

We want our own learning, or that of any student, to be connected, active, and meaningful. But we are also aware of the limitations of time and other resources. Most significantly, we are products of the ways that we were taught, so we often turn first to models that fail to connect. We need, instead, a radical re-creation of curriculum. The examples here provide ideas to inspire that re-creation.

NOTES

1. High school student Nikhil Goyal, "Where American Education Went Wrong," *MSNBC*, September 13, 2013.

2. Alvin Chang, "The Data Proves That School Segregation Is Getting Worse," *Vox*, March 5, 2018.

3. Juan A. Muñoz-Cristóbal et al., "Coming Down to Earth: Helping Teachers Use 3D Virtual Worlds in Across-Spaces Learning Situations," *Educational Technology & Society* 18, no. 1 (2015): 13–26.

4. Jonathan Sacks, *The Home We Build Together: Recreating Society* (New York: Continuum, 2009).

Chapter One

Ecosystems Learning Framework

> The academy is not paradise. But learning is a place where paradise can be created. The classroom with all its limitations remains a location of possibility. In that field of possibility we have the opportunity to labour for freedom, to demand of ourselves and our comrades, an openness of mind and heart that allows us to face reality even as we collectively imagine ways to move beyond boundaries, to transgress. This is education as the practice of freedom.
> —bell hooks[1]

If we take seriously the aim of democracy (as the project of supporting healthy associated living, not a particular governance structure) then we must step back to examine the fundamentals of ideas such as education, learning, and democracy. These terms are used in multiple, often confusing ways. That is not surprising given how much they relate to our personal identity, our hopes for our children and our future, our understanding of social life, our values, and our beliefs.

SOME WORKING DEFINITIONS

Any discussion of education, or learning, that focuses on schools per se prefigures answers to important pedagogical questions. When we study schools and instruction, we emphasize *teaching*, whereas a broader perspective that includes life practices situated in work and community would lead us to talk more about *learning*.[2]

We start with some working definitions, not to end inquiry, but to give it a starting place. First, *learning* is a process of growth, in which an organism (including humans) acquires information, skills, behaviors, and preferences from experience. This experience can often be construed as a failure of some kind; learning enables the organism to cope better with future events. Humans grow in this way, but they also acquire beliefs, values, and habits which enable them to participate more fully and successfully in their social and cultural life.

Education is used here synonymously at times, but often with a distinction to highlight the intentionality of others—friends, parents, teachers, camp counselors, supervisors. *Formal education* usually entails a designated place for learning, such as a school or university, a defined curriculum, and more or less formal organizations and procedures designed to optimize acquisition. *Informal education* can occur within a school, but more commonly in museums, science centers, summer camp, churches, and so on.

However, as classrooms become experiential, place based, collaborative, online, hybrid, flipped, and distributed, and informal settings deliberately encompass curricular goals, such as science, technology, engineering, and math (STEM) education, the formal/informal distinction is hard to maintain.

Many questions remain. Does formal education mean simply what happens in school? Even there, does it mean the intended curriculum, what the teacher or the educational system wants the student to learn, or is it the enacted curriculum, the result of "a complex and multifaceted process, involving different actors and operating at multiple levels."[3] Going further, does education include what students are actually learning through social networks or forbidden practices in school, which may have little to do with the formal curriculum?

Once one looks at the diversity of activities that might fall under these terms, it becomes clear that common images or definitions are not helpful. We cannot get far by defining education as a process that applies to children in school or defining learning as simply acquiring knowledge in whatever way. There are a wide variety of settings to consider—museums, libraries, community centers, clubs, nature centers, work, unstructured play, sports, family time, and online environments—as well as interactions among these. In online environments the distinction between student and teacher disappears, as does a coherent notion of curriculum. And yet learning still occurs, often in purposeful ways.

The narrower view leads us to divides between formal and informal learning, knowledge-focused and community-focused approaches, online and physical spaces for learning, humanities and sciences, self-directed learning and guided inquiry, which dissolve into the mist when we try to grab them. The learning by children, for example, represents an integration of, at a minimum, various experiences in play and daily social life, instruction by parents, and activities in school.

An alternative is the idea of *learning ecosystem*. It gives us a more articulated and nuanced way of talking about the processes of learning, or education. That can be useful in discussing its many practical problems. It can also support work toward education that is more holistic, connected, deeper, engaging, and relevant to daily life. Think of a garden that cultivates the learner throughout the life span.

The *learning ecosystem* approach contrasts with *atomized learning*, whether in formal or informal settings. The latter seeks to identify the fundamental units of learning, such as specific facts and skills. From that basis, the educator's task is to develop criteria for prioritizing among those units, efficient methods of instilling them, diagnostic procedures to assess their acceptance, and remediation where the teaching process fails.

Reducing the learning process to a procedure for acquiring knowledge on isolated topics can be appealing. It is easily organized, described, managed, and tested. But carried to its logical conclusion it obscures purpose, relevance, meaning, aesthetic, and moral development.

In contrast, *ecosystem-based learning* offers a larger perspective on life and education. It can be purposeful, meaningful, social, and integrated with the biological and physical worlds. It grows organically: An activity that starts as a one-off event in a library may continue within homes, then grow to include more partners, find an analogue in the school, and so on, ever becoming. In general, ecosystem-based learning means rich interaction with the world and ample opportunities to reflect and engage in dialogue about those interactions.[4]

It must be noted (and is discussed later in the book) that ecosystem-based learning can also be restrictive and dehumanizing, when the ecosystem does not nurture the learner. Education's ecosystem can include unhealthy practices.

Our working definition for *learning ecosystem* is as follows:

> A learning ecosystem is an assemblage of people and organizations interacting within a dynamic physical, cultural, social, political, and economic environment (family, friends, social roles and norms, buildings, texts, technologies, etc.) to shape growth of the individual and the society.

The learning ecosystem is whatever infrastructure exists for learning, regardless of how effective or how valuable we would judge that learning to be. Within what may be a large assemblage, there are *learning niches* in which learning occurs. These might include online media, books, social interaction spaces, or just an old-fashioned lecture room.

There is an analogy here to adopting a systems perspective toward life on Earth. We learn more every day about the complexity of life and especially the many interactions among its components. We can analyze how biodiversity defines the planet's ecosystems and is shaped by them, or how new ecological niches and properties emerge.

There are negative feedback loops that maintain temperature, acidity/alkalinity, and gas composition within a constant range. The system exhibits resilience deriving from the connections among the components and a complex balancing act among living organisms and the non-living physical world. There can also be positive loops. We are engaged in a massive experiment today to test the biosphere's resilience by rapidly increasing the CO_2 concentration.[5]

In a similar way, the learning ecosystem is more than just a toolbox that enables learning in different modes or media. It can be damaged by removing components or breaking connections among them. Yet, there is also a holistic quality, with emergent properties beyond any specific actions.

EDUCATION'S ECOSYSTEMS

It is widely recognized that we learn through life experiences, that home environments matter for learning in school, and that many lessons in school are quickly forgotten. Nevertheless, the discourse of educational reform is largely constrained to changes that might occur within the classroom. We recognize system-wide problems, but continually revert to solutions involving just one component.

We need a different model. It would

- provide a more accurate account of how people actually learn and teach,
- show how that learning relates to lived experience across the full spectrum of life's activities,
- help us assess and compare different learning ecosystems, and
- help us find better ways to support learning in the classroom but also beyond.

A successful learning ecosystem nurtures integrative learning across many modalities. A deep understanding that we learn through an ecosystem leads to a radical rethinking of how we organize education, and even of what education is.

The ELF highlights some of the key characteristics of this view of life and learning.

1. Diversity in Ways to Learn

A healthy biological ecosystem typically exhibits a high level of biodiversity in terms of genes, species, populations, and ecological niches. We focus here on the diversity among learning niches. A learning ecosystem finds learning occurring in all aspects of life—in work and play, online and off, alone and in social environments, before and after formal instruction. Whereas some might privilege formal over informal learning, or vice versa, the ecosystem perspective seeks to identify the many, diverse ways that we do learn and to account for how different media, modes, and venues for learning fit together and synergistically promote growth.

2. Networking

Not only is there a diverse array of species, populations, and niches, but there is a diversity of ways that they are networked. These connections vary in terms of importance, intensity, redundancy, etc. For example, mutualism describes the ecological interaction between two or more species where each species benefits. By-product mutualism states that organisms cooperate when it is in their individual interests to do so. For example, defending against an enemy for the purpose of self-preservation might benefit another potential prey. Relations such as altruism, reciprocal altruism, and many more make clear that network relations are a vital phenomenon in ecosystems, even though they may be less obvious on first glance than diversity among types of organisms.

A learning ecosystem approach looks beyond a simple additive or substitutive relation among different kinds of learning. Rather than saying, for example, that we learn something about animals through a trip to the zoo, and also something else when we study them formally in biology class, it asks how different modes may complement, amplify, or conflict with each other, how they interact in non-linear ways. The connections among learning experiences become as salient as any individual experience.

It is striking how much of education research does not even attempt to analyze how learning develops in one venue versus another. It rarely looks at more complex relations, such as the social relationships in our homes and cities. Instead, in a misguided effort at scientific control, it often isolates a specific learning experience and tries to explain how it does or does not contribute to a particular learning outcome. A consequence of the interactivity is that it is untenable to think of learning as fitting conveniently into subject matter categories, grade levels, or even formal versus informal settings.

3. Emergent Properties

The interactivity among components leads to *emergent properties*. Properties of the system as a whole emerge, which are not evident when it is considered in terms of its parts. An overall integrity can confer resilience or, negatively, rigidity.

At both its best and its worst, the emergent properties of a learning ecosystem reflect lived experience, not some abstract representation of it. An educational ecosystem thus comprises multiple, diverse, interconnected components with emergent properties. Among many things, there could be the emergence of a love (or hate) for learning. These properties are not always evident on cursory examination.

For example, a group of university students were studying theories of reader response, essentially how the meaning of a text depends on the reader as well as the author, the context, or the text per se. These theories arise in diverse disciplines—philosophy, literary criticism, education, even theology. Their questions grew initially out of frustration at their inability to make sense of these divergent theories.

They tried lining up the theories along various dimensions, eventually constructing a chart, with entries such as "key examples used to represent the theory." The chart was not a definitive summary, but instead a stimulus for further questions, playing a role similar to that of the periodic table in chemistry. Their construction became the site in which their own learning would occur. This was an example of group cognition, in which no one participant, including the teacher, even imagined such a representation in the beginning. It emerged from group activity and dialogue and is the idea from the course remembered most clearly by the students.

4. Finding and Constructing Learning Niches

The house of learning does not have a fixed floor plan, albeit diverse, interactive, and emergent, but one that grows and changes, reflecting the needs and activities of those within. Reconstruction by the participants means that the house of learning is continually reinvigorated. The participants do not simply inhabit or survive within but actively construct and reconstruct their own niches. This mutual constitution of learners and ecosystems is often ignored, especially in the promotion of systems to reform education.

5. Interpretation of Learning Ecosystems

Finally, learners continually interpret their learning ecosystem, making it unique for each individual. Shared conceptions across groups with similar histories can lead to culturally bound practices and interpretations. Whatever properties one person may attribute to that ecosystem, another may see it differently, often in radically diverse ways. Among other things, *interpretation* here includes the fact that how we make sense of something depends on our situation, and especially our history in relation to the history of the other.[6]

DISRUPTIVE POTENTIAL I: ECOLOGICAL INVALIDITY

The fifth characteristic, interpretation, has disruptive potential. In biology, we judge success in terms of reproductive fitness. An organism might think it is doing quite well, it might be happy, but if its genes do not continue in future generations it fails in the evolution game. However, for the study of any human learning situation, the very criteria for success are constructed and interpreted by participants.

This is one reason laboratory studies of learning have limited value. They may reveal properties of the cognitive engine, but what these properties mean must be interpreted in a given situation. But those situations add messiness to a formal study.

For example, we might measure learning of novel material, because we do not want to confound the results by the fact that different participants in the study already know different amounts about the topic, including a variety of misconceptions. But in ordinary life we invariably encounter learning situations with prior knowledge. Similarly, we could simplify things by studying learners in isolation. But people typically collaborate on learning in diverse ways. This collaboration may be fruitful or destructive, but it is a reality of the activity. Performance on a task is also affected by the meaning a person assigns to it, how participants are defined, how different participants interpret it, how it rewards activity, and the meaning of its symbols. Any observer may be led to construe the learning in dramatically different ways.

If we do manage to remove such situation variables from research we end up with a new situation, one that appears only in the lab. This can result in *ecological invalidity*, the condition of having something valid to say about the situation, but not having a justification for applying that elsewhere, in particular to any case we might be actually be interested in. There is no meaningful definition of cognitive skills independent of the environments in which they occur.[7]

The phenomenon of interpretation means that the outside observer is not the only one filling out the ELF. Participants within the situation, including, for instance, teachers, imagine it in ways that make sense to them. They say what the learning spaces are, how they connect, what properties emerge, and what new elements are constructed.

Thus, we need to study natural learning ecosystems, as they evolve. However, our conception of a given ecosystem is shaped by our own interpretation. It needs to be enhanced through a hermeneutic process of uncovering the participants' meanings.

DISRUPTIVE POTENTIAL II: CONTEXT SPREAD

A related issue is that when we apply the ELF, we might like to have a clean research question. For example, we might want to ask about the impact of a new curriculum in a school or what visitors take away from a new exhibit in a museum. We would like for the relevant learning spaces, networking, emergent properties, and construction by participants to be finite. But just as the laboratory psychologist discovers that lab results may be inapplicable beyond the lab, anyone studying a specific learning situation or activity soon finds that other learning activities intrude.

The child who has nothing to eat may be in a learning situation radically different from the one of the well-fed child sitting beside them. This happens even though they both appear to be in the same space at the same time. The encounter that a child has with another on the way to the library may be more salient than the learning activity they experience once they arrive. Issues of personal histories, racism, income disparities, climate disruption, and more can overwhelm the effects of any specific activity.

The consequence of this is that the full application of ELF ought to include everything that might potentially affect the learning. This calls for holistic and interpretive research. Unfortunately, every possible factor means literally everything. Making things worse, regardless of what one discovers, *interpretation* can overwhelm all the other aspects of the learning ecosystem. That is why, in some cases, the most useful analysis is not to list factors, but to be open to whatever the learner interprets as meaningful. This usually entails longitudinal, ethnographic study, or simply listening to the participants' own accounts.

The approach here recognizes that the learning ecosystem is always broader than we can capture in a simple table, or even a multivolume analysis. It is broader than we can imagine. If we proceed with humility, knowing that our analysis is never complete or indisputable, there can be room for a more modest approach to reveal important aspects of the ecosystem and to give us a starting point or a summary of analysis. This can be seen in the following example, where ELF is applied to the Library Parks in Medellín.

APPLYING ELF TO THE LIBRARY PARKS OF MEDELLÍN

The ELF essentially provides a schema for thinking about an educational situation, some questions to ask, and the starting point for assessing or improving that situation. It is not intended to yield a quantitative measure or a step-by-step remedy for problems. As an example, consider how it might be applied in Medellín, Colombia.

The Library Park (*Biblioteca Parque*) idea started there around 2009. These are urban complexes in marginalized communities. It is a good example of learning spaces constructed to support community learning.

Each of the 10 complexes features an imaginative modern building housing a library with computers and broadband access. There is green space all around for walking, play, relaxing, and enjoyment of the architecture and outdoor art. The Library Park becomes the cultural center of its neighborhood, promoting social interaction, educational activities, cultural services, and civic engagement. They combine digital and print media, natural and cultural learning, recreation and scholarship, and local and extended community building.

There are integrated mobility systems with elevated metros, cable cars, bridges, and escalators. A modern transport system connects each Library Park with the others, reducing the isolation of previously disconnected neighborhoods.

The basic idea is to transform disadvantaged communities, improving both the physical and cultural environment. The parks stimulate renewal while promoting civic pride and citizenship development, all under the slogan "the best for the most needy." In these settings, the public library becomes an educational environment emphasizing the social function of education. Participants of all ages develop new forms of reading and writing as political practices that enhance their exercise of citizenship, transforming the public sphere for marginalized minorities (Table 1.1).[8]

The parks provide a network of activity centers promoting education, culture, sport, and recreation. There are diverse spaces for learning (#1),

Table 1.1. ELF Analysis of Learning in Medellín

Learning Feature	Medellín in 1980s	Medellín Today
Diversity	Limited opportunities to learn; invisible territorial boundaries; gated communities	Schools, but also libraries, digital resources, videos, parks, social interaction
Networking	Limited networking, connection to survival skills; marginalized communities	Connections across formal & informal learning, nature & multimedia; promoting social inclusion & participation; bringing the slums & modern life together; linking neighborhoods
Emergence	Violence, alienation	Conception of the city as a whole
Construction	Restricted role for civic participation	Collaboration & integration of professions & disciplines in design; community participation; continual reconstruction
Interpretation	Fear and loss of hope	Urbanism viewed as a tool for promoting social mobility & equity

which interact in positive ways (#2), and there is active participation from community members in the design (#4). One could, of course, go into much greater detail in the analysis, but a first approximation suggests that changes since the 1980s resulted in a healthier learning ecosystem. It also suggests areas in which one might look for more detail, for example, in understanding the interpretations of various participants (#5).

The Library Parks are one reason that Medellín has been ranked as the most innovative city in the world. But a generation ago, life was very different there. In the 1980s, during the drug cartel wars, Medellín was known as the most dangerous city in the world. A child in war-torn Medellín was in danger just trying to attend school and had few other opportunities to learn (#1). This was a negative learning ecosystem (#3), except for learning about survival on the streets.

SUMMARY

The ELF presented here helps to reveal how the learning ecosystem operates in any particular situation. We do not simply accumulate knowledge or skills, particularly not in a single venue or via a single pedagogical approach. We learn through all aspects of lived experience. Crucially, we learn through building relations among diverse life experiences. There are properties that emerge unpredictably from the network of these connections. We find learning niches and construct them, and we interpret them in the light of our prior experiences.

ELF does not prescribe a particular way to teach or learn. It is simply an analytical tool to highlight and help us understand how ecosystems shape learning for good or ill. A useful summary of some known innovations that consider the learning ecosystem but have had limited influence on education is contained in a series of reports from the Open University, United Kingdom. These include playful learning, challenging the legacy of colonialism, learning through wonder, place-based learning, and developing children's social and emotional understanding.[9] There are additional examples in this book of approaches to help ecosystems promote learning in positive ways.

NOTES

1. bell hooks, *Teaching to Transgress: Education as the Practice of Freedom* (London: Routledge, 1994), 207.

2. Jean Lave and Etienne Wenger, *Situated Learning: Legitimate Peripheral Participation* (New York: Cambridge University Press, 1991).

3. Janine Remillard and Daniel Heck, "Conceptualizing the Curriculum Enactment Process in Mathematics Education," *The International Journal on Mathematics Education*, October 2014.

4. In a landmark book on teaching elementary school science, Brenda Lansdown and her co-authors write that all children are born alien: "Could anyone know less about the family, the society, the nation, or the world than a newborn child?" Despite its ignorance, this alien child can learn through a process of investigation and colloquium, talking with others about the meaning they draw from experience. *Teaching Elementary Science through Investigation and Colloquium* (New York: Harcourt Brace Jovanovich, 1971), vii.

5. Lynn Margulis, *Symbiotic Planet: A New Look at Evolution* (London: Weidenfeld & Nicolson, 1998), 120. Margulis uses Gaia as a metaphor for the set of interacting ecosystems on the Earth's surface.

6. This fifth characteristic is the odd member of the list. Most biologists would not include it, or would subsume it under *diversity*. It is, of course, biological, in the sense that we are biological creatures, but it stands out as a distinctive aspect of human activity. The topic deserves more detail than can be presented here. The work of Hans-Georg Gadamer on historicity of understanding, *Truth and Method*, 2nd ed. (London: Sheed and Ward, 1989), is a fundamental resource.

7. Michael Cole, Lois Hood, and Ray McDermott, *Ecological Niche Picking: Ecological Invalidity as an Axiom of Experimental Cognitive Psychology* (New York: Laboratory of Comparative Human Cognition and Institute of Comparative Human Development, Rockefeller University, 1979), 109.

8. Alex Warnock-Smith, "Story of Cities #42: Medellín Escapes Grip of Drug Lord to Embrace Radical Urbanism," *The Guardian*, May 13, 2016; Yicel Nayrobis Giraldo, Gloria Elena Román Betancur, and Ruth Elena Quiroz Posada, "La Biblioteca pública como ambiente educativo para el encuentro ciudadano: Un estudio en la comuna 1 de Medellín," *Revista Interamericana de Bibliotecología* 32, no. 1 (January 1, 2009): 47–84.

9. Rebecca Ferguson et al., "Innovating Pedagogy 2019," Open University Innovation (Milton Keynes: Open University, 2019).

Chapter Two

The Whole Frog

> It is interesting to contemplate an entangled bank, clothed with many plants of many kinds, with birds singing on the bushes, with various insects flitting about, and with worms crawling through the damp earth, and to reflect that these elaborately constructed forms, so different from each other, and dependent on each other in so complex a manner, have all been produced by laws acting around us. There is grandeur in this view of life. . . . From so simple a beginning endless forms most beautiful and most wonderful have been, and are being, evolved.
> —Charles Darwin[1]

Many years ago, on a beautiful fall day, a prospective student walked across the campus at Rice University with one of the best-loved professors. The professor had the lanky frame of Bertrand Russell, completed with a shock of longish white hair. His field was biology, but instead of discussing ecosystems or DNA he expounded about ending war and the need for world democracy. This was heady stuff. The student was engaging in genuine conversation on an important topic with Professor Joseph Ilott Davies.

Davies shared his passion and deeply held beliefs, but also wanted to know what the student thought and cared about his questions. How did a biologist came to care so much about democracy and to see it as an idea to discuss so intently with one of the many young students he must see? How was it central to his life? For me, this question was especially pertinent given what the school ideology of instilling knowledge packaged in simple categories. Shouldn't we discuss plants and animals in biology class, democracy in government class?

TEACHING ORGANISMAL BIOLOGY

Davies had come to Rice in 1914 to serve as Julian Huxley's lab assistant. At that time, he had essentially a working-class occupation, cleaning lab equipment and preparing animals for dissection. But Huxley, who was chair of biology at Rice and who interacted with Nobel Prize winners and international scholars in many fields, became a mentor for him. At one point, Davies wrote a poignant six-page letter to Huxley acknowledging his mentoring. He said Huxley has "made twice the man of me and has put thoughts in my head that I had never dreamed of before; would it surprise you if I thought of trying for a degree at Rice!!!"[2]

While working full-time, Davies enrolled as a student at Rice, receiving his BA, MA, and PhD degrees there. Sometime later, he took over both the classroom teaching and the lab for the introductory course, Biology 100. In that role, he became renowned for his captivating teaching style.[3] It's worth noting that Huxley himself was an ardent internationalist, after his experiences in Germany leading up to WWI. Huxley's role as a caring mentor undoubtedly played a role, but Davies's internationalist views were much deeper and more integrated with both his biology and his teaching than was apparent on that fine fall day.

The first lecture in Biology 100 was always a memorable one. Professor Davies entered the large auditorium and greeted the 200 or so students, all of whom he would soon come to know by name. He then asked, "What is this course about? It's about you. You are many things, and you are each different from one another, but one inescapable fact is that you are all alive. You move, you breathe, you talk. But what does it mean to be alive? How is life possible?"[4]

Davies brought out a large bucket. He reached in and pulled out a living frog. "Look at this beautiful creature. It, too, is alive, but it is so different from each of you. And there is a vast diversity of life you may only dimly understand. How can there be this incredible diversity? What accounts for the common features of life? What accounts for the variations?"

He placed the frog on the lab table in front of him. "Look at how the frog hops. That's one characteristic of its being alive. In this class we will dissect animals and plants to study their systems and organization. But whenever possible, we will study living, breathing organisms, because our goal is to learn more about life, not the parts of life."

He then picked up the frog, perhaps a bullfrog, as in Figure 2.1, and tossed it into the student seating area. There were predictable screams, followed by more screams and laughter, as one student would toss it toward another. Then he pulled out a second frog and tossed it, then a third, and so on, each time asking his questions about life.

Finally, he pulled out the last frog, and along with it a knife. With students watching intently, he chopped through the frog's neck with a single, quick blow. He then released the frog, and it, too, began to hop, without its head.

"Look at this. You saw me kill the frog. We all know that it's dead and that nothing can revive it. Yet it, too, will hop for a short while. Clearly, hopping alone is not what makes something alive, even though most living things do move. As I said earlier, we usually won't kill organisms, but in order to understand life, we will also seek to understand death."

The image is wrenching. In a lecture making the case for life, Davies deliberately destroys it. Whatever else one might say about his teaching approach, or whether torturing and decapitating frogs is ethical, it must be granted that he engaged the students' attention. Students who thought they could not or did not want to learn science found themselves asking questions and engaging in the ideas. Is discomfort a necessary part of learning?

Davies showed in many ways how much he cared for biology, the living organisms who were his students, and even the frogs. Although he was an ardent proponent of biology and a scientific view of the world, his humanism

Figure 2.1.   Bullfrog. New York: American Museum of Natural History, 1900, Wikimedia Commons.

stood out as part of, not in opposition to, his understanding of the physical and biological world. That was reflected in the way his lectures ranged across art, literature, history, and philosophy.

It was also shown in the way he talked about and exemplified a concern for moral values, which he, just like the pragmatists before him, saw as integral to his view of life. His teaching prefigured care theory, as developed by Nel Noddings:

> We do not have to construct elaborate rationales to explain why human beings ought to treat one another as positively as our situation permits. Ethical life is not separate from and alien to the physical world. Because we human beings are in the world, not mere spectators watching from outside it, our social instincts and the reflective elaboration of them are also in the world.[5]

Davies exemplified the idea that "ethical life is not separate from and alien to the physical world." His work was a search for the wholeness that connected these realms and entailed life for the frogs and the students he loved.[6]

GRAND QUESTIONS IN BIOLOGY

The most important impact of that initial lecture was not to convey a set of ideas, but rather to raise one of the grand questions of biology: *How do the various systems of an organism come together into a unified whole to produce life?*

Much of the course then explored the diversity of living organisms and the different ways their systems integrated to produce successful life, for with all their variation and different ways of being in the world, every living organism represents a successful adaptation. Toward the end of the course, Davies focused more and more on other large questions, including what biology had to say about religion, the human soul, and moral codes. His manner of addressing these questions drew as much from poetry and art as it did from biological theory. He even found inspiration from a religious perspective he did not fully share in Cardinal Newman's *Lecture on [Human] Evolution*.[7]

A key theme in the course was the interdependence of living things. Frogs need ponds; we cannot understand one organism without an understanding of the ecology in which it participates. That ecology includes much more than simple competition for resources, but complex and varied means of association. "Life did not take over the globe by combat but by networking. Life forms multiplied and complexified by co-opting others, not just by killing them."[8]

Along these lines, a second grand question became more central as the course neared its end: *How does an individual organism relate to other organisms and to its physical environment?* Davies focused on how the frog relates as one organism to others in its ecosystem. Today, he would have more to say about what is called finding and constructing ecological niches. He would also want to show how the frog itself is an ecosystem, with many subenvironments and comprising multiple species of bacteria, fungi, and viruses. It is itself an "entangled bank."

The features that change a physical space into a biological environment are often constructed by the organisms that inhabit it, notably the creation of an oxygen-rich atmosphere by plants. Even more fundamentally, what *counts* as significant cannot be disentangled from the needs and activities of the organism. Instead, we need a view of organic evolution as a constructive process.

The idea of the continuity of life points to a third grand question: *How does an individual organism relate to its history?* Histories are individual, as we see in the processes of development and aging. But they are also properties of the community and the population. Every living thing is a product of its parents and those who went before. History shapes those who are to come. Relations through time complement relations of organisms to the physical world and to other organisms. This idea was reflected in the course through investigations of the histories of organisms.

Together these grand questions about the wholeness of individuals, the ecology, and continuity opened up for students a complex inquiry into the variety and processes of life. Like Darwin, a century earlier, their inquiry was situated in wonder about the beauty of life. For better or worse, Davies's course turned many students on to biology and directed some away from it, at least the part involving killing animals.

DAVIES'S OWN ECOSYSTEM

Two years after Davies and the student talked about humans learning to live and work together, he announced his retirement. In May of 1966, he gave the last lecture for Biology 100 that year and what was to be his last lecture after a lifetime of learning and teaching biology. Former students, colleagues, and people from all over could not stay away. It is difficult to say how many people attended, probably double the approved capacity of the already large auditorium. Many were disappointed not to get inside.

Davies spoke with his familiar passion for learning and exhibited his continual caring for students. Although he had aged, he seemed to stride across the stage and speak with more energy than ever before. At the end, there was a standing ovation for a man who had risen from lab assistant to professor and had devoted his life to learning and community. There was only one question: What will you do now? Davies paused, then replied that he did not know; perhaps he would travel some.

A short time later, after Davies delivered his last lecture, he died while grading final exams. During his life, Davies had diverse interests, including photography, literature, architecture, and philosophy. But he was devoted to biology and to helping his students grow. Thinking about what made his life a unified whole, about its ecology and its history, it is difficult not to feel that the end of teaching meant that his life was severed and that he had lost some of the essential wholeness of life.

Some small solace may be found in the George Eliot selection he shared during his "Lecture on Evolution": "Oh, may I join the choir invisible / Of those immortal dead who live again / In minds made better by their presence."[9] Davies interpreted this as follows: "To me, these are grand thoughts. They take some of the sting out of death by recognizing nobility of character during the life of the individual. They lessen the void of death by accentuating and perpetuating through new lives those virtues for which the individual was revered while he lived."[10]

SEEING THE FOREST

Davies's insistence on studying the whole, live frog did not extend in practice to field studies. But conceptually his approach implies learning about frogs not only as intact, living organisms, but creatures in complex interaction with a whole ecosystem. That perspective is increasingly seen as vital for understanding any organism.

Suzanne Simard's research on forests shows that trees have evolved to *participate* in interdependent relationships with fungi and other trees. They *communicate* within and across species. They also *cooperate*, sharing nutrients and warning signals. And they help *create* their own ecological niche. Simard's work complements the thesis that symbiosis, cooperation, and creation are as important for evolution as competition.[11] She writes:

> All trees all over the world . . . form a symbiotic association with belowground fungi . . . [which] sends mycelium, or threads, all through the soil, picks up nutrients and water, especially phosphorus and nitrogen, brings it back to the plant, and exchanges those nutrients and water for photosynthate [a sugar or other substance made by photosynthesis] from the plant. . . . In a natural forest of British Columbia, paper birch and Douglas fir grow together in early successional forest communities. They compete with each other, but . . . also cooperate . . . by sending nutrients and carbon back and forth through their mycorrhizal networks.[12]

The work on tree talk reminds us that we can attain only a limited understanding of organisms if we conceive them entirely as isolated individuals, or study them only in hothouse environments or laboratories. Just as an organ within a plant or animal makes sense only when considered in the context of the needs and activities of the full organism, key aspects of an organism can be understood only in their relationship with other organisms and the physical environment. Symbiosis among organisms is a fundamental fact of life science.[13]

Peter Kropotkin articulates a more complex view in his classic anarchist text, *Mutual Aid*, which was also *a prescient text for studies of ecology*. Although supportive of Darwin, Kropotkin's observations led him to question the bitter struggle for existence, which many of Darwin's followers considered to be the main, if not the sole, factor in evolution. Arguing for naturalistic studies, Kropotkin writes that when we study animals "not in laboratories and museums only, but in the forest and the prairie, in the steppe and the mountains—we at once perceive . . . mutual support, mutual aid, and mutual defence."[14]

In recent years, these and more complex forms of interaction among species have become more widely recognized. For example, the One Health approach recognizes that human health is connected to the health of animals, plants, and their shared environment. There are even more complex interactions among the members, activities, spaces, and values just within a human community.

ECOSYSTEMS

An ecosystem is a network of organisms living along with nonliving components, interacting as a system through nutrient cycles and energy flows. Plants incorporate energy through photosynthesis; animals feed on plants, breaking down organic matter; decomposers convert nutrients stored in dead biomass back to a form that can be used by plants and other microbes. In an ecosystem, abiotic factors are mutually constituted with the biotic. For example, temperature and rainfall influences where and how different plants and animals live; organisms also influence temperature and rainfall, as anyone can see in a cool, moist forest.

A *(biological) community* is an interacting group of various species in one location, competing for survival. An example community is a forest comprising plants from ground cover to tall trees, animals, mosses and lichen, and soil containing bacteria and fungi. A community might include several *populations*, or groups of organisms of a species that interbreed and live in the same place and time. The standard view of *ecosystem* is that it is a community of interacting organisms along with their physical environment. The physical environment is often assumed to be fixed and given, an empty space in which the community operates.

This standard view has not been supplanted, but it has been complicated in a number of interesting ways in recent years. The physical environment is no longer fixed and given, but a much more dynamic process of energy flows and nutrient cycling. Notions of emergent properties for assemblages of organisms, mutual aid among both animals and plants, communication and sharing of nutrients through mycorrhizal networks, cytoplasmic symbiosis, rhizome reproduction, and the construction of ecological niches have led life scientists to focus on relations among organisms and assemblages, as a vital new unit of analysis. They see ecosystems as more complex and dynamic than ever before.

BIOLOGIC AND LEARNING ECOSYSTEMS

New ideas from life sciences, including cooperation among and across species, the construction of ecological niches, and the need to see environments in terms of the activities of organisms, show that evolution is not simply a race to the top among isolated individuals, with only the winner destined to survive. Instead, it tells us that life flourishes within a complex set of relationships among diverse species and habitats, giving and taking, sharing and competing, communicating, growing. These are ever changing, in part because they are actively constructed, reconstructed, and interpreted by the participants.

The ELF applies to both biological and educational fields of interaction. In the case of the frog, we can examine the diversity of organisms and their habitats. We can study the connections among these and the properties that emerge out of complex networks. We can also see how frogs construct their own ecological niches and interpret them.

We should resist reducing education to a biological system. Nevertheless, there are many parallels. Learners show diversity in their backgrounds, interests, abilities, and motivations. Similarly, their learning niches can be very diverse, especially when one looks beyond the school. The connections among these become the field in which education occurs. Learners also construct and interpret their learning spaces.

One can see the analogy more clearly through consideration of cases in which the system breaks. For example, frogs are endangered because of habitat destruction, pollutants, disease, and other stresses. The consequent loss of organismal and habitat diversity may be irreparable. In education, we can threaten the possibilities for growth by reducing the diversity of learning niches and the opportunities to learn. The education ecosystem shapes our capacity for *formative justice*, how we choose to form our lives.[15]

A challenge in ecological studies is to define concepts such as habitat, biodiversity, invasive species, or healthy ecosystem. We should not expect it to be significantly easier to do the same for education. Yet we need to recognize that an ecosystems perspective can help us determine the important questions to ask.

Just like the frog, we are more than the sum of our biological parts. Our life depends upon complex interactions within our bodies and with other organisms, including both competition and cooperation. Like the frog, we shape and interpret our own environment. We also have special reflective and communicative capacities. Our model of learning needs to recognize that we learn in diverse parts of our ecosystem and, most importantly, through connections among our experiences. These connections are vital for an integral education.

SUMMARY

This chapter presents a sketch of life sciences, which have increasingly adopted a systems perspective on the cell, the organism, the population, and ecosystems. Biologists have recognized the amazing diversity of life and habitats, and of the network of interactions among these. These phenomena are mirrored in education's ecosystems.

NOTES

1. Charles Darwin, *On the Origin of Species by Means of Natural Selection* (London: John Murray, Albermarle Street, 1859), 490.
2. Nancy Boothe, "New Huxley Archive Provides Unique Documents," *News from Fondren* 7, no. 1 (September 1, 1997): 5.
3. Sara Meredith, "Unforgettable Joseph Davies," *The Flyleaf* 1, no. 2 (1966): 1–6.
4. The quoted material represents paraphrases based on Davies's lecture notes, the articles about him, and the author's memory. They show the sense of dialogue he conveyed, albeit in a lecture format.
5. Nel Noddings, *Caring: A Feminine Approach to Ethics & Moral Education* (Berkeley, CA: University of California Press, 1984), 187; Maurice Hamington and Ce Rosenow, *Care Ethics and Poetry* (New York: Palgrave Pivot, 2019).
6. The course said little about the molecular basis for life. Although the research on DNA inspired many at the time, it was still quite new and difficult to incorporate into a course with a long history. Moreover, as the course was designed for nonmajors, it did not assume a deep understanding of chemistry and physics.
7. Joseph I. Davies, "Biology 100: Lecture on Evolution," *The Flyleaf* 16, no. 4 (July 1, 1966).
8. Lynn Margulis and Dorian Sagan, *Microcosmos: Four Billion Years of Evolution from Our Microbial Ancestors* (Berkeley, CA: University of California Press, 1997), 29.
9. George Eliot, *O May I Join the Choir Invisible! And Other Favorite Poems* (Boston: D. Lothrop, 1884).
10. Joseph I. Davies, "Biology 100: Lecture on Evolution," *The Flyleaf* 16, no. 4 (July 1, 1966), 13.

11. Joan Roughgarden, Martin Nowak, and many others contribute in this area, too much to cover here.

12. Suzanne Simard, quoted in Diane Toomey, "Exploring How and Why Trees 'Talk' to Each Other," *Yale Environment 360*, September 2016.

13. Lynn Margulis, *Symbiotic Planet: A New Look at Evolution* (London: Weidenfeld & Nicolson, 1998).

14. Peter Kropotkin, *Mutual Aid: A Factor of Evolution* (Montréal, Québec, Canada: Black Rose Books, [1914] 1989), 5. Mainstream biology downplays Kropotkin's views, or similar ideas about group selection, because the mechanisms are not evident, it is difficult to study complex interactions in the field, and individual selection is usually a more parsimonious explanation.

15. Robbie McClintock, "Formative Justice: The Regulative Principle of Education," *Teachers College Record*, September 27, 2016, 1–38.

Chapter Three

Why Do We Educate?

> We must remember that intelligence is not enough. Intelligence plus character—that is the goal of true education. The complete education gives one not only power of concentration, but worthy objectives upon which to concentrate. The broad education will, therefore, transmit to one not only the accumulated knowledge of the race but also the accumulated experience of social living.
> —Martin Luther King Jr.[1]

Many a child in school has asked why they have to be there. The answer is not always clearly evident. Why does education happen at all? This chapter considers the contemporary standard view (CSV) as an answer to that why question. It then summarizes some of the major problems from multiple perspectives. From there it moves to alternatives, leading to the ecosystems perspective.

THE CONTEMPORARY STANDARD VIEW OF THE AIMS OF EDUCATION

Many people in the West, especially in the modern era, would say the foremost reason for education is that it prepares young people to get a good job; the more education, the better (i.e., the higher paid that job can be). This is the economic, or the professional, justification for education. The career focus has grown, both because workplace demands have increased in complexity and to accompany a reduction in the focus on moral education found in earlier religious schools.

The focus on career often precludes other goals, such as learning how to understand the perspective of others, critical thinking, and service to society. Success is defined as quantifiable improvement on micro-testing quantifiable bits of knowledge and skills. This leaves little room for developing aesthetic capacity, reflection, integrative understanding, and other characteristics of human flourishing, which might enable democratic participation.

In a distant second for most is the aim of learning how to participate as a citizen in a democratic society. This includes specifically becoming a responsible citizen, but more broadly learning how to get along with others, listening, understanding different perspectives, discussing ideas effectively and peaceably, and avoiding violence. This is the political, or social, justification.

Some, most often those comfortable economically, identify a third aim, human flourishing, including developing one's potential as a reader, appreciating arts and literature, developing physically, and such, essentially learning how to self-actualize and to enjoy a good life.

The CSV identifies three main aims for education—to earn a living, to become a good citizen, and to develop latent powers to enjoy a good life. These are complementary.[2] For example, through work we also learn how to communicate and to understand the perspective of others, essential skills for one seeking to be a productive citizen of a democracy. Moreover, those skills help us develop our latent powers, as we learn about our self through work and learn from others. Similarly, developing our latent powers and faculties can help us to earn a living or be a responsible citizen.

Progress toward achieving one of the aims can clearly further progress on another. But they can also be in conflict: Equipping young people to make a living may succeed at the cost of preparing them for a life of drudgery, very far removed from enjoying a rich and nourishing life. The time spent on vocational pursuits may alone mean there is less time available for discussions of citizenship, morality, or aesthetics.

PROBLEMS WITH THE CONTEMPORARY STANDARD VIEW

The prevalence of the CSV (to earn a living, to become a good citizen, and to develop latent powers to enjoy a good life) in school mission statements, education textbooks, and other documents does not mean that it is a coherent position. There are conflicting definitions of education itself and the relative importance and meanings of work preparation, citizenship education, and humanistic education.

Moreover, nearly every word in the aims has multiple and conflicting meanings. Does "earn a living" mean simply attaining any job? Does it mean equal opportunity for every student to obtain the highest status or best paid jobs, or is it primarily to serve the interests of local employers for specific skills needed in their industry? Is it the same kind of job for one starting out rich as for one starting out poor?

There are several larger problems with the CSV. First, it is committed to a narrow cognitive frame, in which knowledge is primarily represented in texts. It leaves to the student the major challenge of connecting that formal knowledge with body, friends, work, nature, or other aspects of lived experience.

Another problem with the CSV is that it leads to education that for many is hollow, inert, and disconnected from lived experience. The development of latent powers typically garners little attention, and is often reduced to reading required literature, not necessarily a bad thing, but a limited proxy for nurturing full human potential.

Moreover, the CSV is excessively individualistic. It fails to appreciate the embedding of the individual in groups, cultures, and society. Education certainly has functions for the individual, but it has largely been instituted for societal aims. A central activity of societies around the world has been to educate the young, and sometimes, those not so young. That happens wherever society needs to pass on its accumulated knowledge and especially its values to its citizens. It is often for a select few, and where more broadly applied, differentiated, especially across gender and class.

Education serves to reproduce society, to accomplish its aims. This is where things become complex since there are a diversity of views on what those aims should be. They could include democracy, human flourishing, uncritical consumerism, blind obedience to rulers, racism, or nationalistic fervor leading to xenophobia and war.

Education can provide a corrective to society, not reproducing it, but challenging it. A paradox is that society resists the challenges that education can make to its ground assumptions, but it relies on education to change those assumptions if it is to survive. James Baldwin describes the paradox as follows:

> What societies really, ideally, want is a citizenry which will simply obey the rules of society. If a society succeeds in this, that society is about to perish. The obligation of anyone who thinks of himself as responsible is to examine society and try to change it and to fight it—at no matter what risk. This is the only hope society has. This is the only way societies change.[3]

Despite the historical linkage of schools and society, the CSV leads us to conceive schooling as an activity separate from life outside the school. In a similar way, a college of education operates independently of the nutrition department in the college of agriculture, the department of criminal justice, the business college, the department of sociology, or other departments that have much to say about education. The relationship between school and society never disappears, but the relation can be obscured. Activities are carried out because they have always been part of the curriculum or the school day. A parent may come to school to talk about her work as a microbiologist, but the science curriculum is unaffected by that visit.

This general separation is reflected in the separation of subject matter: science from humanities, math from art, literature from social studies. If what students study in the classroom is kept independent of practical life, then it matters less if the knowledge is disconnected.

It usually takes a catastrophe, such as the shooting that occurred in 2018 at the Douglas High School in Parkland, Florida, to break this glass wall. Not only did the outside world intrude in a horrific way on school, but the students soon became the central organizers of the most powerful grassroots gun-reform movement in nearly two decades. But when students do think beyond their local social concerns, they find that that the typical formal curriculum provides little help in addressing issues such as access to weapons, extreme political divides, mental health, income inequality, the changing workforce, or other issues that relate to their concerns.

The solutions that many people advance, such as adopting innovative education technology, focusing on new skills, changing what knowledge is imparted, restructuring the grade levels or classroom formats, improving teacher education, etc., are usually seen as operating within the school system as it is. They modify the operation of the school but do not change the relations between it and the larger society.

The education system as a whole, in contrast with an individual teacher, professes all of these aims, but then it happily ignores them. The focus narrows to the first component of the CSV (career preparation). Assuming without much evidence that cognitive performance is the key to job success, the system then works to engineer a process in which student achievement on narrowly specified cognitive measures exceeds that of other schools (districts, states, countries, past exam takers, etc.). It uses those measures to evaluate students, teachers, schools, districts, states, and nations. Accordingly, education is continually reformed to produce better results on those measures.

For example, the (US) No Child Left Behind Act (2002) mandated testing to identify failures to progress, where "progress" was interpreted to be measurable by performance on standardized tests. Later, the Every Student Succeeds Act (2015) became the first federal law to require that all students be taught to high academic standards to prepare them to succeed in college and careers. These and similar policies in the United States and elsewhere essentially define the education process as one of producing outputs in terms of test scores, justified by a purported link to economic success.

CRITIQUES OF CONTEMPORARY EDUCATION

Since education is central to life, criticizing it is a popular pastime. There is endless fodder: from concerns about specific school test scores or the testing regime per se, a particular teacher, an example in a textbook, the vacation schedule, standards of dress and decorum, equal access, even the school bus route.[4] The criticisms are many, and from diverse quarters.

A major criticism from those who see education as career preparation is that it fails to do precisely that. Although ostensibly central to life, it is oddly disconnected from the daily life that most people know. The curriculum is too often impractical or out of date. It appears to prepare students for jobs that no longer exist, or never did in proportion to the corresponding studies.

Many argue that the system is self-referential. Like any organism, it seeks to perpetuate itself and its own importance. Thus, it emphasizes preparation for extending studies rather than to life beyond the school. Correspondingly, there is limited support for lifelong learning. The school appears to say that you must learn the prescribed set of facts, whether they give value or not, then leaves you on your own for applying those facts in life itself.

Schooling is inevitably antiquated. There is a long lag between recognition of the importance of some phenomena, such as new communication technologies, medical research, environmental studies, or space science, and then its incorporation into formal studies. It takes years for that phenomenon to be deemed important, and more still for it to replace some previously anointed topic. A long process is required to reduce it to a manageable bite for the curriculum, translate it into textbooks and lectures, add it to exams, and otherwise make it part of the educational system. By then, the once-new ideas have become obsolete, while newer ideas are left out of the system.

There is often little on computing, which is striking in an era of social media, virtual reality, and big data. Entrepreneurship, whether of the get-rich kind or social entrepreneurship, is rarely found, except sometimes in higher education. The arts, which were once considered essential, have been systematically removed. A consequence of these omissions is that any critically engaged student realizes that much of what they need to learn must come outside of school.

Through obsolescence and timidity, education is disconnected from the major issues of the day: climate change, biodiversity, globalization, racism, economic justice, housing, substance use, violence, changing family norms, sexuality and sexual relations. Students begin to feel that school discourse is about one set of issues, which they see as hollow and uninteresting, while the issues they care about are ignored, if not banned from discussion.

Consistent with the omission of ethical and political discourse, there is a lack of nurturing of moral development. Moral development and civic education often appear only in severely truncated forms if at all. Modern secular education abandons the ancient Greek idea of *arete*, used most often to imply an inextricable link between excellence in learning and moral virtue. Arete is essentially the act of living up to one's full potential as a good and knowledgeable person. But morality is often avoided in academic discussions, given a context of competing visions of the good and the difficulty of assessing it in the modern drive toward quantifiable educational progress.

Meanwhile, despite abundant evidence of the benefits of physical activity for physical and mental health, and even overall academic success, schools are reducing physical education classes and recess time.[5] This happens for reasons of cost, liability, and lack of equipment, but also the unsubstantiated belief that time spent away from formal studies risks lowering test scores, the dominant measure of educational success.

There are also huge inequities in resources and access to education, between and within nations. The problems mentioned above are moot for those who have no access to learning at all. Many in the United States are less concerned with the educational critiques above than with simply gaining access to safe and decent schools. They ask why their school has poor facilities and lesser prepared teachers. Why is it shut down when there are educational challenges, rather than being given extra resources and attention? They also ask why college and many kinds of technical training can be on the required path to success, yet economically out of reach.

These issues lead to an unsurprising alienation of students, and often teachers, parents, and citizens. A consequence of the separation of school from life is that school exists for many of us in a virtual realm of its own. The idea that real life is found somewhere other than in school is an unacknowledged assumption. In *The Teenage Liberation Handbook*, Grace Llewellyn tells young people that quitting school is the way to get a real life and education.[6] One does not have to accept her recommendation to realize that many of the teenage readers she is addressing experience this distance. For them, school lacks meaning, because it seems to have nothing to say either to their immediate concerns or to their long-range plans.

Debates about the success of education are compounded by disagreements about the relative importance of different goals, such as job training versus enlightenment, and how to measure progress toward those goals. But there is an added complication: Many of the goals are inherently contradictory.

Instilling obedience, and an unquestioning respect for authority and tradition, as some might advocate, is fundamentally at odds with developing a critical consciousness and learning how to transform society. There are many less obvious and partial contradictions, too, such as that between learning scientific facts and scientific attitudes. It makes no sense to argue over methods absent some clarification of purpose.

GANDHI'S RESPONSE

Adopting a societal, cultural, and political perspective on education in South Africa and India, Mahatma Gandhi worked toward a radically different conception of education. He described the three, notably Anglo aims of education (the CSV) as part of a colonial project of subjugating people. He not only rejected those aims; he also developed specific alternatives.

For example, Gandhi agreed that it was important to develop the mind, but when that effort was divorced from development of the body and the spirit, education was at best incomplete and more often oppressive. He considered the British system to be overly focused on cognitive goals and then only as they enabled job performance:

> The real difficulty is that people have no idea of what education truly is. We assess the value of education in the same manner as we assess the value of land or of shares in the stock-exchange market. We want to provide only such education as would enable the student to earn more. We hardly give any thought to the improvement of the character of the educated. The girls, we say, do not have to earn; so why should they be educated? As long as such ideas persist there is no hope of our ever knowing the true value of education.[7]

He did not ignore career preparation, but he saw the necessity of integrating it with moral development and cultural relevance. It must also be done with the aim of political empowerment toward developing a just society. Gandhi was shocked by the conditions of women working as virtual slaves in the mills of Bombay. As an alternative to preparing them for that work, or other similar roles in the colonial system, he promoted traditional handweaving in schools.

Gandhi describes education as development of the mind, body, and spirit. True education requires a proper exercise and training of the bodily organs (e.g., hands, feet, eyes, ears, nose, etc.): "A proper and all-round development of the mind, therefore, can take place only when it proceeds *pari passu* with the education of the physical and spiritual faculties of the child. They constitute an indivisible whole."[8]

The connection to traditional work naturally complemented Gandhi's emphasis on *learning by doing*. Through meaningful work with dignity, the individual would learn to think creatively, independently, and critically. Furthermore, the emphasis on work culture would accord with his view of service to society as a higher goal. He essentially supplanted the Three Rs of the British system with a focus on head, heart, and hand, later recapitulated in the U.S. 4-H program.

Despite his insistence on service, work, cultural relevance, and other connections to the human ecosystem, Gandhi did not by any means reject learning from books. In his *An Autobiography*, he describes his own encounter with a book (John Ruskin's *Unto This Last*) "that brought about an instantaneous and practical transformation in my life." There, he discovered some of his deepest convictions, especially about the good of the individual being contained in the good of all, the value of all work, and that the life of labor is the one worth living.[9]

Some of these points can be summarized in an ELF analysis of education in Gandhi's time (Table 3.1). Gandhi shows that, whatever aims we adopt, they cannot be considered in isolation from the society in which education is embedded. Equipping a young person to play a part as the citizen of a democracy has very different demands for one in an already functioning democracy or in a colonial position. It also has quite different meanings according to economic class or race, and gender.[10]

Consider a simple gardening example: Learning how to make compost for a garden may require knowing how to assemble a container using various tools. It certainly requires some knowledge of what materials are biodegradable and which plants would benefit from extra nourishment. It might require knowledge of temperature, moisture, sunlight, and other physical factors. It may draw upon aesthetic considerations regarding how to design or place the composter, or social concerns, such as collaboration. It might be relevant to consider the cultural practices and values of the community, or the historical tradition for gardening in the area. Even that simple task calls up the larger ecosystem of learning.

However, in conventional schooling, and particularly in the British colonial model, potentially relevant disciplines, such as mechanics, biology, physics, art, and psychology, are all taught happily without concern for integrating with each other or with action in the world.

Table 3.1. ELF Analysis of Colonial Education versus Gandhi's Program

Learning Feature	Colonial Education	Gandhi's Program
Diversity	Learning from lectures and reading	Traditional work as part of schooling, service to community, etc.
Networking	Little connection to daily life	Connections across formal & informal learning, explicit links to cultural practices
Emergence	Predefined outcomes	Political empowerment
Construction	Imposed on colonial subjects	Citizens as creators of their school & society
Interpretation	Divergent interpretations by British rulers and Indian or South African subjects	Schooling seen as key to nation building, preservation of culture, political freedom

CULTIVATION

An early justification for education and a program for what it should be comes from Confucius (551–479 BC) and the tradition in which he was embedded. He and his followers viewed education as *cultivation*. This suggests biological growth, which may include but is not reducible to acquisition of specific knowledge and skills, as the modern, technocratic vision of education appears to do.

Flourishing growth for an organism, and its active counterpart, cultivation, has for millennia been the traditional Chinese view. The development of virtue, broadly defined, was a goal for life and hence for schooling. Taoists proposed achieving internal moral integrity as a desired state of quiescence. They all agreed that human capability and competence could be enhanced as virtue was pursued. Cultivation is a lifelong process supported by the educational and social structures of society.[11]

There are three key aspects to the idea of cultivation. First, just as a gardener needs to attend to all parts of a plant and to its various needs for light, moisture, temperature, physical support, and so on, a teacher needs to focus on the whole person—knowledge and skills, virtue, aesthetic development, physical growth, unique characteristics, and so on. Second, there is a focus on growth and development throughout life, from the earliest days to the end, with schooling as one part of the process. Third, social structures are needed to support and reinforce values and the education process. Learning is primarily a social process.

Cultivation identifies the purpose as developing virtue as central to the ideal of a person who serves society. The metaphor is gardening, not stacking up bricks. The cultivation perspective presumes that we learn in a social environment. Our transactions with others define when, where, how, and what we learn. We have the capacity to learn how to act justly, and we do so by acting in a just way. Learning to be a good citizen is part of individual development, not something to added on later.

Although the Chinese view of education as cultivation is ancient, it holds promise as a theoretical model for ecosystem-based learning. The core ideas can be seen in the Western thread on education as natural growth, evident in Rousseau and Pestalozzi. For example, Friedrich Froebel likens education to the trimming of a grapevine, for which the gardener needs to attentively follow the nature of the plant.

He notes that "we give time and space to young plants and young animals, knowing that they then beautifully unfold." We let them rest and protect them from powerful influences. But we treat the young person as "a piece of wax, a lump of clay, from which he can mould what he will."[12]

In his dying days, Froebel urged care for his garden, asking that friends take care of his flowers and spare the weeds, because he had learned much from them.[13] Weeds taught Froebel that active hindrance or constraints for a learner could hamper their growth, but that in a natural state they reveal their pure inner life. Froebel's kindergarten would demonstrate that of the best ways to give time and space for young children to unfold is to encourage them to learn through observing and nurturing plants in a garden. The gardening notion led him to coin the name kindergarten, an approach that greatly influenced early childhood education around the world.[14]

The cultivation approach sees the primary purpose of education not so much to equip or prepare students for particular tasks, but instead as organic growth, enabling them to live fully. Imagine a plant in the garden. The gardener waters, fertilizes, and perhaps guides it to grow in its unique, only partially predictable way.

Dewey argues that growth for the child comes from full engagement through living in association with others and with connection to diverse forms of life. The growth perspective is essential but it is not simply unfold-

Figure 3.1. Studying, Growing, Harvesting, Selling, Preparing, and Enjoying Food (Nisarga Batika School, Kathmandu, Nepal).

ing, because human growth depends on social relations and participation in social life. This is why the ecosystem is so important; an empty space does not provide the rich network of connections to physical, biological, and social life that are needed.

Consistent with the idea of embedding learning in an ecosystem is that learning should include forms of life that are worth living for their own sake: "Education is a process of living and not a preparation for future living. . . . The school must represent present life—life as real and vital to the child as that which he carries on in the home, in the neighborhood, or on the playground."[15]

Dewey's classic formulation for this is "We always live at the time we live and not at some other time, and only by extracting at each present time the full meaning of each present experience are we prepared for doing the same thing in the future."[16] Learning how to live fully and extracting the full meaning of each experience enables each of us to acquire knowledge, develop our bodies, participate as a citizen, define a moral compass, enjoy a good life, earn a living, or whatever other goals we may assume.

DEMOCRATIC EDUCATION

Education and democracy are highly interdependent.[17] Like education, democracy requires a faith in human experience. That experience becomes "lived" when we extract meaning and apply that meaning to live more fully in the present. This process, the process of education, provides the basis for ever-renewed social life, and hence democratic living.

Late in his life, Dewey makes the case for democracy as a never-ending educational process. Contacts, exchanges, communications enlarge and enrich experience. These interactions must be carried on daily; democracy fails when these are restricted just as an ecosystem suffers when its networks are severed or reduced.[18] Education and other institutions of democracy must be continually renewed, strengthened, and connected to one another. Knowledge of social arrangements and how to improve them thus become central to schooling.

A glaring contradiction is that increasing segregation of schooling by race and class[19] means that schools cannot provide opportunities for students to learn directly what it means to live and work with others whose daily lives are different from themselves, a condition that is essential for democratic life.

Democratic education is thus both an end and a means to sustain democracy. It is an end when we conceive democratic life as a primary goal of education. Community cannot be an optional afterthought; it needs to be a fundamental guide to action. Robert Starratt describes this as making community "an explicit, intentional, and programmatic component of the school curriculum."[20] In that case, community is not just a way to organize learning; it is the thing which needs to be learned: The community is the curriculum.

Interest in the community as curriculum idea has grown in recent years because of concerns about the fragility of communities coupled with awareness of their value as a resource for learning.[21] It is inspired by a recognition of the limitations of formal education, in contrast to more traditional situated learning and how communities of practice support learning even in advanced industrial societies. An implication of this is that democracy and democratic education are not two loosely related processes, but two sides of one process.

A further consequence is that the practice of democratic education both requires and leads to transformation of individuals and organizations. This transformation implies a change in perspective: Learning about democracy needs to be seen as much more than learning about procedures, or even community service. Instead, it is what Doug Schuler describes as cultivating *civic intelligence*. He envisages networked groups working within their own communities and across traditional boundaries using new communication and information technologies as appropriate. The civic sector then becomes a force capable of consciously and pragmatically constructing more intelligent capabilities.[22]

For Harry Boyte, cultivating civic intelligence leads to a different kind of politics: "The creation of public spaces can be a seedbed for productive, pluralist, citizen-owned politics in an age of gated communities and privatized resources." To do that, we need to understand education as a process of transformation, the "reworking" of ourselves and our contexts.[23]

The examination of society was central to the progressive education movement in the United States, a movement that recognized explicitly the democratic mandate for schools. It developed in the early twentieth century, during a time of massive immigration to the United States, rapidly changing information and communication technologies, the shift to knowledge work, and concerns about building a democratic society. There are precursors of that movement, similar projects internationally, and continuations today.[24]

One key element of progressive education has been the goal of developing a "critical, socially-engaged intelligence." A second key element is a respect for diversity in all its forms—whether by gender, sexuality, physical ability, religion, ethnicity, race, class, or nationality.[25] This is essential, not only to have a fair and just society, not just because it maximizes the possibility of learning for all, but also because democratic life means including all citizens in the process of authority. Respecting each member of society, or, for that matter, each student in a classroom, means realizing that each has unique experiences, and thus knowledge that could and should be heard, shared, and drawn upon to address contemporary problems.

This perspective of democratic education suggests that the first objective upon which to concentrate is understanding our lived experience in the world, including all of the different ways we relate to it. We might suppose that lived experience in a distilled form is exactly what makes its way into textbooks, curricula, and teaching approaches. However, political and economic forces, and simply the power of time and distance, estrange those aspects of formal education far from the experience of the learners.

At the same time, learners' experiences are ignored, and before long, the life of the school becomes distant from the life of the student, and from the community. It no longer serves to transmit "the accumulated experience of social living." Instead, the prevailing tendency has been to conceive education as career preparation and to judge schools and universities on the basis of graduates' employment prospects and salaries.

Cecelia Tichi shows how the social conditions of the progressive era led reformers to social activism in areas of working conditions, health care, economic opportunity, and shared governance; educators responded in a similar way. She argues further that in the United States today there is a pressing need for a renewed progressive response.[26]

How do we assess social conditions and whether they should be maintained or changed in some way? Can we make our communities and the larger society work? King's College London, for example, has adopted the United Nation's Sustainable Development Goals (ending poverty and hunger, promoting gender equality, working for sustainability, etc.) as a measure of the university's success. That goal at least recognizes the interdependence of formal schooling and its surrounding ecosystem, that each must work to sustain the other.

LEARNING COMMUNITIES FOR ALL

The best teachers are also inquiring learners. An example can be seen in a study of Physics Van, which travels to K–8 schools to show that science is fun and helps in understanding how the world acts as it does. A middle school English teacher in one evaluation study saw connections between the inquiry process in physics and the writing process she teaches to her students. But, more importantly, she said that the experience was important to her professionally, because it validated her sense of herself as one who can learn new things. It reinforced her reasons for entering the profession in the first place, and the daily practice provided too little of that.[27]

A leader of progressive education, Lucy Sprague Mitchell exemplified critical social engagement through her commitment to collaboration and inquiry for both students and teachers.[28] Building upon the examples of both Jane Addams and Dewey, she cofounded what eventually became the Bank Street College of Education. She saw the need for her students, future teachers, to develop an inquiring attitude toward work and life:

> Our aim is to turn out teachers whose attitude toward their work and toward life is scientific. To us, this means an attitude of eager, alert observation; a constant questioning of old procedure in the light of new observations; a use of the world as well as of books as source material; an experimental open-mindedness; and an effort to keep as reliable records as the situation permits in order to base the future upon accurate knowledge of what has been done.

Rejecting the dichotomies of science/art, teacher/learner, and reason/passion, Mitchell also called for nurturing creativity in all its forms:

> Our aim is equally to turn out students whose attitude toward their work and toward life is that of the artist. To us, this means an attitude of relish, of emotional drive, a genuine participation in some creative phase of work, and a sense that joy and beauty are legitimate possessions of all human beings, young and old. If we can produce teachers with an experimental, critical, and ardent approach to their work, we are ready to leave the future of education to them.[29]

If an important goal is to develop "teachers [and students] with an experimental, critical, and ardent approach to their work," then pedagogy cannot be a simple rule-driven procedure. Nor can the process be easily assessed through standardized tests. How would we measure a sense of joy and beauty? All participants must have the opportunity to ask questions; to investigate through reading, observation, and participation; to create; to collaborate with and learn from others; and to reflect on their experiences.[30]

Learning communities need to include teachers, but they often do so in the most limited sense. Chris Higgins details how typical working conditions for teachers include shabby, inadequate facilities. There is a general disregard for all teachers exacerbated by racist disregard for students and teachers of color. The racist hierarchy infantilizes teachers. There is crippling isolation and few opportunities for professional advancement.[31]

He argues that just as the professional ethic for teachers seeks *eudaimonia* (flourishing) for their students, it must also encompass the needs, desires, aspirations, and welfare of practitioners themselves. Good lives for students, for teachers, and for citizens in the society at large are all deeply interdependent. From this perspective, inquiring teachers must become inquiring learners as well.[32]

SUMMARY

Education operates across multiple spaces, reflective of the activities and purposes found there, and exhibiting properties akin to those of a biological ecosystem. Thus, the processes of education and of learning overlap. This contrasts with the CSV that learning is the acquisition of knowledge and education is systematic instruction to achieve that. Theories as diverse as those of Gandhi, Confucius, and early Greek philosophers offer alternatives to that CSV. Although they differ in significant ways, these alternatives share a concern for the ecology of education and for learning as a process of holistic growth, not simple knowledge acquisition.

It may come as a surprise to learn that the ecosystem perspective actually brings the teacher to a more significant role in learning. In conventional teaching the teacher essentially delivers prepackaged knowledge. Much of that task can be accomplished via video, animations, online simulations, databases, and programmed learning modules. Many teachers do much more than this. But the system as a whole is designed to focus on, then assess, the transfer of well-defined structures of knowledge in the most efficient way.

In contrast, the ecosystem perspective positions students as teachers and teachers as learners. It calls for dialogue and collaboration in a complex environment, entailing a more complex response from any teacher. As learners become more self-reliant they are simultaneously more in need of collaborators. They especially need experienced others who can provide scaffolding for learning, serving as models, interlocutors, facilitators, guides, and critics.

Like a biological environment, the school is not an empty space, but a dynamic environment constructed by the organisms within. It exists within and in relation with other environments—home, work, play, and so on—and cannot be understood separately from them. Successful education cannot be only about some hypothesized future, or other life. Even if children could thrive to some extent through activities in a hothouse environment, we would not know how well they were equipped for life outside of that. If our goal were to understand learning, we would learn little of much use.

A corollary is that if our goal were to promote learning for the individual to participate in the world beyond the school, we need to ensure that the school environment connects with and reflects the world. For example, if we want students to develop a scientific attitude toward life, we need to ensure that they actually do science, and that they do it in areas that are meaningful to them. Otherwise, we are not providing experiences that help them thrive beyond the school.

NOTES

1. From King's first published work, "The Purpose of Education," *The Maroon Tiger*, January 1, 1947, 10.

2. C. E. M. Joad discusses these aims and their complementary in a classic, *About Education* (London, UK: Faber & Faber, 1945). T. S. Eliot considers the interrelation of aims and the conflict among them in *To Criticize the Critic* (New York: Farrar, Straus & Giroux, 1965). The threefold formula is similar to a later one in Mortimer Adler's *The Paideia Proposal: An Educational Manifesto* (New York: Simon & Schuster, 1982).

3. James Baldwin, "A Talk to Teachers," *The Saturday Review*, December 21, 1963, 42.

4. Gloria Ladson-Billings, "From the Achievement Gap to the Education Debt: Understanding Achievement in U.S. Schools," *Educational Researcher* 35, no. 7 (2006).

5. Harold W. Kohl et al., *Educating the Student Body: Taking Physical Activity and Physical Education to School* (Washington, DC: National Academies Press, 2013).

6. Grace Llewellyn, *The Teenage Liberation Handbook: How to Quit School and Get a Real Life and Education* (Rockport, MA: Element, 1997).

7. M. K. Gandhi, *Gandhi on Education*, ed. J. S. Rajput (Urbana, IL: National Council of Teachers of English, 1998), 3.

8. Ibid., 73.

9. M. K. Gandhi, *An Autobiography or The Story of My Experiments with Truth*, trans. Mahadev Desai (Ahmedabad, India: Navajivan Publishing House, 1927), 275.

10. Samuel Bowles and Herbert Gintis, *Schooling in Capitalist America: Educational Reform and the Contradictions of Economic Life* (Chicago: Haymarket Books, 2014).

11. Shihkuan Hsu and Yuh-Yin Wu, eds., *Education as Cultivation in Chinese Culture: Education in the Asia-Pacific Region: Issues, Concerns and Prospects* (Singapore: Springer, 2015).

12. Friedrich Froebel, *The Education of Man*, trans. W. N. Hailmann (New York: D. Appleton, 1887), 8.

13. Bertha von Marenholtz-Bülow, *Reminiscences of Friedrich Froebel*, trans. M. H. Mann (Boston: Lee and Shepard, 1892), 29.

14. Michael Steven Shapiro, *Child's Garden: The Kindergarten Movement from Froebel to Dewey* (University Park, PA: Pennsylvania State University Press, 1983).

15. "My Pedagogic Creed," in *The Collected Works of John Dewey, 1882–1953* (Carbondale and Edwardsville, IL: Southern Illinois University Press, 1967), EW 5:87.

16. Dewey, "Experience and Education," LW 13:29–30.

17. Dewey, "Democracy and Education," MW 9:4–370.

18. Dewey, "Creative Democracy: The Task before Us," LW 14:229; Dewey's point that democracy is an ongoing, never-ending project is carried forward in Richard J. Bernstein, "2000, Creative Democracy—The Task Still Before Us," *American Journal of Theology & Philosophy* 21, no. 3 (September 2000): 215–28.

19. Jason M. Breslow, "The Return of School Segregation in Eight Charts," *PBS Frontline*, July 15, 2014.

20. "Community as Curriculum," in *Second International Handbook of Educational Leadership and Administration. Part One*, ed. Kenneth A. Leithwood and P. Hallinger (Boston: Kluwer Academic Publishers, 2002), 321.

21. Jim Cummins, Patricia Chow, and Sandra R. Schechter, "Community as Curriculum," *Language Arts* 83, no. 4 (2006): 297–307; Jeannie Oakes and John Rogers, *Learning Power: Organizing for Education and Justice* (New York: Teachers College Press, 2006).

22. Doug Schuler, "Cultivating Society's Civic Intelligence: Patterns for a New 'World Brain,'" *Information, Communication & Society* 4, no. 2 (June 1, 2001): 157–81.

23. Harry C. Boyte, "A Different Kind of Politics: John Dewey and the Meaning of Citizenship in the 21st Century," *The Good Society* 12, no. 2 (2003): 12.

24. Mustafa Yunus Eryaman and Bertram C. Bruce, *International Handbook of Progressive Education* (New York: Peter Lang, 2015).

25. University of Vermont, "A Brief Overview of Progressive Education," John Dewey Project on Progressive Education, January 30, 2002.

26. Cecelia Tichi, *Civic Passions: Seven Who Launched Progressive America (and What They Teach Us)* (Chapel Hill, NC: University of North Carolina Press, 2011).

27. Bertram C. Bruce, Michael Weissman, and Michael Novak, "Science Education Outreach: Physics Demonstrations, Lectures, and Workshops," *Spectrum: The Journal of the Illinois Science Teachers Association* 23, no. 2 (Summer 1997): 8–12.

28. Joyce Antler, *Lucy Sprague Mitchell: The Making of a Modern Woman* (New Haven, CT: Yale University Press, 1987).

29. Lucy Sprague Mitchell, "A Cooperative School for Student Teachers," *Progressive Education* 8 (January 1, 1931): 251.

30. Bertram C. Bruce, "Building an Airplane in the Air: The Life of the Inquiry Group," ed. Joni K. Falk and Brian Drayton (New York: Teachers College Press, 2009), 47–67.

31. Chris Higgins, *The Good Life of Teaching: An Ethics of Professional Practice* (John Wiley & Sons, 2011), 200–202.

32. Catherine T. Fosnot, *Enquiring Teachers, Enquiring Learners: A Constructivist Approach for Teaching* (New York: Teachers College Press, 1989).

Chapter Four

Diversity in Ways to Learn

> Teachers can increase the academic achievement of students from diverse groups if they make use of, and build upon, the knowledge, skills, and languages these students acquire in the informal learning environments of their homes and communities. . . . Most of the learning that occurs across the life span takes place in informal environments.
> —James A. Banks et al.[1]

There are millions of species of organisms on Earth, of which fewer than two million have been officially named.[2] Many organisms are small, including microbes inhabiting almost every corner of the land and sea. There are phytoplankton in the ocean, fungi, worms that build soils, insects that pollinate specific plant species, and of course the multicellular plants and animals, including fish, birds, reptiles, amphibians, and mammals.

Some of these are producer species using photosynthesis or chemosynthetic processes; others are consumers that depend for sustenance on energetic biochemical compounds generated by the producers. "From tiny viruses and bacteria, unrecognized for millennia, to blue whales weighing 200 tons, and fungi that spread for hundreds of hectares underground, the diversity and extent of life on Earth is dazzling. In its life and reproduction, every organism is shaped by, and in turn shapes, its environment."[3]

Those nooks and crannies for life include deep sea vents, the interior of rocks, frozen tundra, hot sand deserts, and much more. No one has even attempted to enumerate the number of environments. Both organisms and their environments are continually being created.

Life on earth is fantastic, but the corner inhabited by people may be the most fantastic of all. The diversity of organisms and environments is far surpassed by the variety of human experiences, across cultures, languages, music, arts, forms of work and play. This leads in turn to the many types of learners and the environments they inhabit. Our educational ecosystem means that we learn in an amazingly diverse set of ways.

Learning occurs in a variety of environments. Schooling, especially public schooling that brings together people from diverse backgrounds, is a vital part of that, but it is still only part. In fact, formal schooling occupies only a small portion of the life span. Even while engaged in the years of formal education, most of our learning happens elsewhere. We experience both *lifelong* and *life-wide learning*. Learning is ubiquitous.[4]

Even within school, the intended learning activities are more diverse than often recognized. They include lectures, discussions, recitations, work on problem sets, collaborative group learning, free reading time, interactions online, and hands-on activities. Also, the learning that does occur within school may be a consequence less of the intended curriculum and more of social relations, play, sports, screen time, or simply growing up. Sayings such as "experience is the best teacher," "the school of hard knocks," and "learning on the job" remind us that much of what we learn is from participating in parts of the ecosystem beyond the area labeled as school, but also that experiences within school are more than they seem.

This chapter explores the diversity of learning and the multiple environments for learning that can be found by peering into one small corner of life. Other elements of the ELF—networking, emergent properties, construction of learning niches, and interpretation—are present as well, but it stands out first as highlighting the diverse niches for learning within the ecosystem.

THE BAHAL

In Patan, Nepal, adjacent to the capital, Kathmandu, there are many courtyards, squares surrounded by small businesses and residences. There is usually no traffic other than the annoying, unavoidable motorbikes. One of these courtyards is near the Kumbeshwar Temple complex. There are a dozen or so four- to six-story buildings surrounding the small area called Dhumbahal Square. In many ways, the courtyard (or, Newari, *bahal*) is similar to a courtyard in London or in some older U.S. cities, except that those typically have well-groomed bushes and trees, walkways, and convenient benches. They offer a peaceful respite from city life.

This courtyard in Patan is Darwin's tangled bank, a different story entirely. Within 100 feet square, about the same size as the average U.S. suburban lot—one quarter acre—there is more to see than anyone can absorb. A Buddhist stupa on one side defines the space. Around the perimeter one finds a communal water source, a small Hindu *mandir*, a tiny shop that miraculously produces any item you can name, a beauty parlor (and training center), a motorbike wash and repair center, a weather station on top of one of the buildings, and other establishments.

Water is brought in by truck to fill large, black plastic tanks on the top of each building. That water becomes the tap water, getting its pressure from the height of the tanks. It is filtered, but most people drink bottled water for safety if they can.

Activities

The ground is covered about a third with bricks. Some of those form a sort of patio; others are arranged in a curving pattern as if they knew exactly where most people would like to walk. There are also a slate paved area, some concrete, lots of bare ground, and amazingly a little grass. It is not clear why one surface is in one place rather than another, but it all seems to work. As remarkable as some of these objects may be, it is the activities around them that cause one to watch, mesmerized. Each of the activities are opportunities for learning.

A woman tosses millet in the air to remove chaff; another takes an offering with candles and flowers to the temple; a man splashes water on the ground to reduce the dust; boys roll an abandoned motorcycle tire around the stupa as two girls walk around the same monument turning the prayer wheels; a young man washes his motorcycle; an older man gets an open-air shave and haircut; a young couple take endless photos of their young child; women hang laundry and water flowerpots; children play rock-pitching games. It's notable how often fathers are caring for children. One older boy (twelve years old) runs to pick up a younger one (six years old) who's fallen. He comforts him and brushes the dust off his pants. The children also sing and dance.

Meanwhile, there is construction. Patan may be the oldest city in the Kathmandu Valley, dating back more than two millennia, and the bahal is in one of its oldest parts. However, there's a feel of new building everywhere. Some of this is needed reconstruction after the damage of the 2015 earthquake. But workers are building new apartments, too, reflecting early gentrification of the area.

One man digs a mystery hole that ends up being eight feet deep with surprisingly straight sides. Later, small boys use the dirt from the hole as a site for play and the uncovered rocks for their pitch and toss games. A small crew puts up a cell tower, without using any harnesses or visible safety equipment. The construction goes on amid the young children playing, older ones coming and going from school, adults working and relaxing. But a crowd gathers to study the hole and to watch the construction. There is much talk, questioning, and formation of hypotheses about it all.

Observing this is like watching a complex movie, except one that is showing 360 degrees around, with sights and sounds, but also with tastes and smells, touch, heat and cold. There is no beginning to the bahal's day; one moment segues into the next 24/7. A dog may start barking at 2 in the morning and soon have dozens of others to talk with. Sometime around 5 in the morning is an important inflection point.

It is then that the first temple bells are rung—one is deep and loud, two are middle volume, but one of those is high pitched. There are several smaller ones, too. If the dogs aren't already going they soon make up for lost time. Motorcycles start up. Human voices come in, conversing rapidly or yelling. Before long children are running and squealing about. In little gaps, one can hear pigeons cooing, crows cawing, and songbirds singing. The roosters manage to make themselves heard above it all.

This continues throughout the day, although each hour has its distinctive character. There are sounds of children laughing, singing, and squealing at play from the nearby school. There's even a time in the afternoon when all but one dog decides it is too much trouble to bark anymore. That one gives a few desultory yaps, but his heart is not in it. In the evening, dinnertime chatter percolates all around, and later, Nepali pop music. Figure 4.1 shows an example of music in daily life and learning.

One day, the signature event was a wedding. Although it seemed to involve most of the bahal and many visitors, it didn't stop the other activities. There was a 50-foot-long tent being erected and red plastic chairs being set up in rows. Soon, a 14-piece band appeared. There were of course many photos, of babies and children and women in beautiful saris. There were also a number of young men in what must be called dandy outfits and poses.

On first encounter, the chaos of the bahal is disturbing—too many scary dogs snarling; too much noise; too many strange sights, sounds, and smells; too many chances to trip on rocks or broken pavement. But the bahal is actually a very safe place, away from the street traffic and noise, and where people know one another.

Punctuation to Daily Life

There are diverse religious observances. Some people walk clockwise on the path around the Buddhist stupa. This is known as taking *pradakshina*. They turn the prayer wheels as they go. Others perform daily *puja* (a prayer ritual performed by Hindus) in the home or in the bahal's small Hindu *mandir*. There are special pujas to mark festivals or lifetime events such as the birth of a baby or a wedding. One learns a little of the rules of cricket by watching a game with improvised wicket, ball, and bat, similarly the procedures of motorcycle repair establishment or the beauty shop.

Diversity in Ways to Learn 45

Figure 4.1. Music in the Bahal, near Kathmandu.

After a while it all, or most of it anyway, begins to make sense. There are patterns and relations that fit into a larger whole. One child loves to talk in a mix of Nepali and English; another speaks Newari; yet another seems too shy to say anything. The apparent chaos is actually welcoming, enriching, overcoming difference. There's peace in the bustle that is less apparent in quiet solitude. It reminds one of the (anonymous) saying, "Peace does not mean to be in a place where there is no noise, trouble, or hard work. It means to be in the midst of those things and still be calm in your heart."

Place-Based Learning

In contrast to the school experience of the children living there, bahal life represents an opportunity for place-based learning with *real stuff*. The learning is contextual and draws upon emotional and physical responses. It is a living museum that complements the structured activity of the school.

Learning in the bahal is similar to what Ann Lewin identifies in a very different context for learning, a different ecological niche. She writes about how children's museums in the United States differ from typical classroom learning.[5] Yet her analysis applies to the bahal as well.

First, in a children's museum, learning begins with *hands-on* experiences. Visitors learn directly from exploring an entire house cut in half, shopping and staffing a Mexican market, cuddling live animals, interacting with giant objects 12 times normal scale, and making huge soap bubbles. Flipping the usual classroom order, hands-on comes before or even supplants text-based learning. Learning is thus *embodied.*

This is the case for bahal life learning. It is in fact more hands-on than the learning in any museum. Keeping the museum metaphor, children construct their exhibits. They improvise a game of cricket, using a concrete post as a wicket, a discarded stick as a bat, and small rocks in place of a ball. They create another game in which a human chain defines a safe space. Their bodies are the real stuff of their activity. They play with animals in the bahal—dogs, cats, and the occasional cow.

They often shoot a rubber band chain onto the stupa. This is a good game except that the chain often hangs up out of their reach. They can climb the lower part of the stupa, but the upper part is too steep and slippery; it is a smooth concrete dome. Also, there are many electric wires that can catch the chains. The game becomes a complex problem-solving activity—designing different forms of chains, inventing tools for launching them, and then devising innovative ways to retrieve them.

A second characteristic of children's museums and bahal life learning is that, in contrast with the typical classroom, the learning is informal. It is structured by a *space frame*, not a time frame. Participants stay with an exhibit or activity as long as their interest lasts, rather than according to the school bell or the semester schedule. Learning is *embedded* in the physical space and structures of daily life.

This is amply evident in the bahal. Children move from stupa to mandir or from the fountain to the mystery hole. Most of all they respond to people in the bahal, the women preparing meals or washing clothes or dishes, the men working on motorbikes, the visitors passing through.

Third, these venues support *learning in context*. A museum may create a space, such as an entire Japanese house. Events within that context support richly textured learning, with multiple cues to connect with other experiences. The experience is holistic, multidisciplinary, and relatable to the real world beyond.

This is even more true for bahal life learning. It has the holistic characteristics found in a good museum, but it is even more connected to the work of the community, in this case the motorbike repair, the beauty shop, the grocery, and home life, the real life as the children know it. Learning is *extended* across other people, objects, tools, and spaces.

Finally, there is conscious attention, or just space, for the visitor's *emotional response*. Lewin says that a child, or an adult, may experience curiosity, puzzlement, or even fear. They are invited to appreciate beauty and to be awed by the complexity or unpredictability of objects in interaction. These emotions are natural components of learning, helping to make ideas memorable and learning enjoyable. The intellectual and the emotional in human activities are divided by convention, not by fundamental difference.[6]

Emotions are always a key aspect of bahal life as well. They are mostly happy ones, but also include fear, anger, and hurt. Thus, the learning is not always enjoyable. It also has a strong embodied component. The children are continually moving, learning with and through their bodies.

This comparison shows how different bahal life can be from the school that the children attend. It is closer to the activity of the best children's museum. But it goes further. It is constructed by the children, rather than being designed for them. It is more physical, to the point of being dangerous. Most significantly, for the children, the activities provide fun and escape and are not done to achieve a curricular goal.

What Do They Learn?

Participating in bahal life, if only by observing it, allows one to learn many things. Consider just one example of many: The mystery hole leads to much examination and vigorous discussion about its purpose. About a week after it appears, workers insert some kind of flat cable. This is attached to the cell tower several stories higher. A conversation with the workers confirms that the hole and cable are for grounding the tower against possible lightning strikes. Of course, one could read about these experiences, but the opportunity to be there is both motivating and essential to understanding.

Beyond those onetime events, children (and adults, too) learn about social interaction, responsibility, and the lives of others. They learn about the work of their neighborhood, effectively beginning a process of apprenticeship. They learn about plants and animals, religion, language, the properties of materials, and physical laws. They learn these things in a situated way that has meaning for their lives. Of course, its very situatedness means that it is difficult to abstract or generalize that knowledge for transfer to other situations.

Each child (or adult) in the bahal acquires unique life knowledge interacting with the complex ecosystem of the bahal. At the same time, they acquire abstract knowledge, from parents, in school, through reading and dialogue with others, which helps them manage the diversity of possibilities bahal life presents to them.

Connecting to Formal Learning

It is difficult to observe the bahal life without some regret that it is so disconnected from formal learning. The children there mostly enjoy school, but it clearly takes second place to playing in the bahal. This raises many questions: Could the school be organized so as to support hands-on, contextualized, space-based, and emotional learning? Alternatively, could the activities within the bahal be more of a resource for building the school curriculum?

There are many examples of possible connections. Consider just one. The erection of the cell tower was a multiday event that captured the attention of the bahal residents. It introduced many phenomena that could stimulate learning—the operation of cellular networks, the physical demands of building a tower strong enough to withstand winds and rain, the role of the mystery hole, the nature of electrical circuits and grounding, the economic and political dimensions of the cellular industry.

But even without any intentional connection, the bahal life shapes life in the school. Children build their friendships through the bahal play. They talk with each other, with parents, and with visitors about school life and other matters. The discourse is multilingual, including at a minimum Nepali, Newari, and English. As a result there is much talk about talk, which informs the learning of Nepali and English in school.

Similarly, school life shapes bahal life, by extending vocabulary, valorizing concepts and theoretical perspectives, and occasionally referring directly to experiences in the bahal. A proper education ecosystems analysis needs to examine what happens in the school, in the bahal, and elsewhere, and how they connect in a larger system of growth. Table 4.1 shows a first step in that analysis of the ELF.

Real Stuff

One inescapable characteristic of bahal learning is that it involves real stuff. This stuff derives from work in the community, such as preparing vegetables, repairing motorcycles, or cutting hair. It also reflects found objects, which are re-created or reinterpreted to meet social needs, for example, using discarded lumber and a concrete pedestal to make a cricket court.

Learning there is tied to tangible objects with color, texture, elasticity, weight, smell, and taste. This is in sharp contrast with the classroom for the bahal residents, where learning starts with abstractions. Words written on a blackboard or in a textbook describe a physical world, but they demand a leap of imagination for the student to see that world as real. The consequence is that the young people experience two kinds of learning: One is deemed "important," but it feels hollow and distant; the other is not even recognized

Diversity in Ways to Learn 49

Table 4.1. ELF Analysis of Learning for Children in the Bahal

Characteristic	Bahal Life	Neighborhood School	System Comprising Bahal and School
Diversity	Situated, embodied learning; multiple venues (hair styling, motorbikes, cricket, etc.) with serendipitous events, such as the cell tower	National curriculum represented in textbooks & lesson plans; codified knowledge beyond the local, representing historical, disciplinary, & cross-cultural modes of inquiry	Already shaped by bahal dialogue & experiences; could be more productive through a stronger appreciation of bahal life learning
Networking	Connections through friendship & familial networks, but little explicit reflection or integration	Subjects of study well integrated within (e.g., the math curriculum), but not connected well to each other or to outside-of-school life	Potential for making school learning more relevant & challenging, connecting with the bahal & other city life, but difficult to implement
Emergence	Nurturing & child care	New curricula based on network of English schools in Kathmandu	Unrealized potential
Construction	Invention of games	Student art projects	Perhaps based on a funds of knowledge approach
Interpretation	Children seeing the bahal as their home	Schooling as activity separate from life	New conceptions of the nature of knowledge and schooling

as learning, although all would agree that it is engaging, self-motivating, and fun. A closer look would show that it does indeed lead to valuable learning.

A three-part solution seems obvious: Find ways to change the classroom to become more engaging, and more real to the students; recognize the learning that does occur in the bahal; and, possibly, connect the two. As a start, could the richness of bahal life be brought into the classroom (or library, museum, community center, etc.)?

One approach can be found in the work of Gladys Spencer.[7] Over seventy years ago she developed a remarkable list of audio/visual (A/V) materials for use in schools and libraries. One is tempted to ignore her list, since it is at best severely dated, and at worst simply lists some obvious and boring media, maybe filmstrips and posters.

But Spencer's list highlights the many ways in which we learn. She includes the usual, for that time, items such as maps and charts, but she also lists specimens from nature, field trips, and dramatic performances. Her idea is that students can learn through audio and visual presentations, such as we see through the World Wide Web today, but that they also need experiences involving taste, smell, touch, and the kinesthetics of their own bodies, and face-to-face interaction with other people, especially when those experiences are connected to the physical environment. Learning, even in the classroom, should be experiential and embodied. It should also be embedded in daily life and extended through connections to other people and real stuff.

This is just a small sample of the items she includes. Today, each item on her list would have a dual interpretation, as a potential application through the Web, and as something that cannot be duplicated. For example, one could argue that the Internet dance. Among other things, one can

- observe dances from around the world;
- see those dances in stop action, slow motion, or diagrammatically;
- find music to accompany dance;
- share videos or commentary on dances;
- create avatars who dance;
- experience a virtual or augmented reality of dance; and
- dance with people around the world using hologram projections.

In these ways, the Internet can be an invaluable supplement to the study of or experience of dance. However, a classroom or a curriculum that did not create a space for actual dancing, both conceptually and literally, would present a severely circumscribed idea of what dance means, and the experience for the learner would not have crucial aspects of touch, smell, and kinesthetics. The same goes for most of Spencer's other items. The Internet offers a version of or an enhancement to each of them. But in every case, the multimedia version is limited without its embodied complement.

Diagrams showing the variety of resources available through the Internet and arguments about how these will transform education, work, and social life have become familiar. As wonderful as these may be, they also highlight our increasing estrangement from the stars overhead, plants and animals, the artifacts that populate our living and work spaces, deep engagement with other people, and even our own emotions and bodies.

Spencer's list is interesting on its own, as a re-envisioning of what A/V materials can mean. But it also suggests ways to bridge across realms of learning—daily life as in the bahal, structured informal learning as in a museum, the Internet, and formal classrooms. Without such a bridging, daily life can remain episodic and unreflective, while more structured learning becomes meaningless, disconnected, and hollow.

In a 1932 essay on the aims of education, Whitehead decries the focus of the traditional curriculum on "inert ideas," which are disconnected from present use and from each other: "The result of teaching small parts of a large number of subjects is the passive perception of disconnected ideas, not illumined with any spark of vitality." Instead of teaching many subjects, "from which nothing follows," we should recognize life as the sole subject matter for education. Whitehead points out that women who had been denied formal education in his time actually learned more than those subjected to it. Their experiences by midlife made them the most cultured part of the community.[8]

A generation earlier, Jane Addams makes a similar point. She argues that household tasks keeping women out of the public realm afford them knowledge needed for excellent city leadership. Men's military conception of government should be replaced by public housekeeping based on lived experience: "The very multifariousness and complexity of a city government demand the help of minds accustomed to detail and variety of work, to a sense of obligation for the health and welfare of young children, and to responsibility for the cleanliness and comfort of other people."[9] Thus, experience, learning, and responsible civic participation are inextricably linked.

Embodied, Embedded, Extended Cognition

An examination of life in the bahal and of Spencer's A/V list reminds us that learning cannot be reduced to formal symbol manipulation, as modern curricula, even online approaches, often do. Advances in artificial intelligence have revealed that aspects of the mind are like an advanced computer, but they have also highlighted that the mind does not operate independently of the body, or the social and physical worlds. The further that technology progresses, the more evident it becomes that intelligence, artificial or natural, is inseparable from its ecosystem. Our hands (and feet, eyes, ears, noses, etc.) are part of our intelligence. They are what connects to the situation in which we are embedded and shape our thinking as much, or more than, any logical processing.

Recent cognitive science has developed a new conception of cognition that departs from the heretofore dominant Cartesian view. As the bahal makes evident, our thinking is embodied, embedded, and extended. Alva Noë says we are part of the world and not in our heads; we are patterns of engagement with other beings and stuff.[10] This view makes cognition less an individual activity, and less what fits with the connotation of "mental."[11] The new conception is vital for learning ecosystems.

First, cognition is seen as *embodied* because it depends on aspects of the agent's body other than the brain. In early Greek philosophy, the idea of embodied cognition was a commonly held view. The gymnasium was used for exercise and communal bathing, but also for scholarly discourse and learning. Rhetorical, athletic, and musical training were deeply interrelated through a network of overlapping practices, all of which were "bodily arts." Rhetorical training was then an embodied practice, not simply the acquisition of abstract knowledge.[12]

As epistemology developed as a discipline, especially after Descartes, knowing was reduced to abstract, disembodied conceptions. Arthur Bentley describes this as using the human skin to demarcate knowledge from the world. He argues that mainstream philosophers view "knowledge as a capacity, attribute, possession, or other mysterious inner quality of a 'knower'; they view this knower as residing in or at a 'body'; they view the body as cut off from the rest of the universe by a 'skin.'"[13]

The essential interdependence of cognitive and bodily learning can be seen in the clinical work of Alexander. He saw that undesirable, but unconscious, habits were exacerbated in the moment of performance. A speaker's voice would begin to raise in pitch and speed, a musician would miss notes, a skilled dancer would suddenly become clumsy, or an ordinary person would slump in a chair. When Alexander tried to help, he found that the old, wrong way felt right to the client, especially at the moment of performance; the improved way felt wrong. As a result, the client could learn in a mechanical way, but would fail at the moment they most needed to apply their knowledge, for example, when asked to speak to a crowd.

Out of these insights, Alexander developed a technique for deliberately halting a wrong action and consciously applying directions to stop the old habit. The momentary pause, or "inhibition," gave him the ability to change himself and later to teach others to do so. Dewey became an avid follower of the Alexander Technique because it demonstrated for him the unity of mind and body. It was a revelation to discover that thought could be applied to everyday movements as well as to what he had thought of as purely cognitive pursuits. Moreover, thinking with the whole body could be crucial for what seemed otherwise like abstract thought.[14]

Second, cognition is *embedded* because it is distributed across the thinking agent and the physical, social, and cultural environment.[15] This can be seen in Leo Casey's research with adults who desired but lacked digital literacy. Many felt seriously disadvantaged, experiencing the lack in both embedded and embodied ways. One forty-five-year-old, "Ben," perceived himself to be on the edge of the digital world.

Ben lived in Dublin, but one day embarked on a travel adventure in Paris. There, he met a woman in a bar. She shared her email address and he later wanted to write to her. Not having his own computer or smartphone, he decided to use the coin-operated public access point in the lobby of the hotel. But this became a frustrating and embarrassing encounter.

Ben could not cope with either the hardware or the software of the system. As Casey says, he is "right up against it, almost despairingly, trying to break through."[16] For Ben, his cognition, his learning, are inseparable from his social and physical circumstances and from his bodily situation, including his age, gender, experiences, identity, and physical needs.

Although competent in other areas of work, Casey's informants are undermined by the introduction of new technology. This is a special problem since digital literacy is increasingly important for participation in everyday life. They feel left behind and alienated.

All learning is embedded in the physical, social, and cultural environment. That is true in the relatively controlled setting of the school, but even more as we look at learning with a broad compass. Saying that learning is embedded is another way of saying that participation is essential.

This is why education cannot be defined solely in terms of constructs such as a formal curriculum, scope and sequence charts, or instructional guides, and needs to be seen instead as an embodied activity. This is painfully the case for the child who is hungry, but also evident in the ways that participation is shaped by gender, race, disability, and other factors. It is inherent in the role of the arts for learning. It also applies to the chemistry student whose clumsiness causes him to mishandle delicate lab experiments.

Third, cognition is *extended* because it goes beyond the boundary of the individual organism to include others, people to be sure, but also potentially other living organisms and even artificial intelligence, through distributed cognition.[17] Ed Hutchins goes further to say that the "scene" itself has cognitive properties of its own, distinct from those of the individuals who participate within. His examples include modern Western ship navigation in contrast with traditional methods practiced in Micronesia.

The crew of a ship can function as a distributed machine, in which the cognitive burden of ship navigation is offloaded onto various members of the crew. Study of this "cognition in the wild" shows not only the effect of culture on individual cognition, but also the cognitive properties of the cultural activity system itself.[18] The cognition is *extended* across the physical, social, and cultural environment. It also represents another sense of *embedding*.

MIND, BODY, AND SPIRIT

Knowledge was never an individual attribute, but the shift from apparent individual learning to group cognition has become evident through the Internet. It overcomes physical distance and facilitates collaboration among all sorts of groups. Global networking enables even narrowly defined interest groups scattered around the world. Education is extended through collaborative learning, and of course language, which shapes and is shaped by learning activities.

This separation from the natural, physical world of our bodies is especially detrimental for young children. Our knowledge is based on our experiences of our bodies interacting with their environments. Even the vocabulary of our thinking is grounded in this.[19] We develop our bodily senses and skills through interaction with the physical environment.

While the Internet partially supports the idea of extended cognition, it does less well with embodied and embedded cognition. One could argue that a nature webcam helps us become more in touch with our embodied presence in the world or that a location tracker reminds us of our embedding in city life. Ironically, despite ample claims to the contrary, new information and communication technologies offer disconnected experience at the time when we are becoming most aware of the importance of connections to one another and to the natural world.

The three Es (embodied, embedded, and extended) as well as similar notions, such as *enacted*, all point to the importance of *participation* in daily life. Learning is enabled by, and shaped by, the ways we participate, whether this is participating with our bodily, sensuous, and aesthetic self, with the biological and physical world, or with other sentient beings. This shift in perspective about cognition accords with the view that any aspect of the community can become a site for learning.[20] Ties to family, friends, work, play, and daily life in the community provide a rich substrate for situated learning.

SUMMARY

Education is part and parcel of an ecosystem with physical, biological, cultural, social, and political aspects. Everything we learn can be traced back to aspects of the ecosystem of which we are a part. And as we are increasingly aware, our survival depends on being able to apply our learning to preserve that ecosystem for future generations.

If the curriculum is based on life as we know it in the neighborhood, region, or world, learning becomes more relevant. Students can see the connection between their individual lives and larger social concerns such as care for the environment, cross-cultural understanding, or understanding world heritage.

When learning grows out of concrete lived experience, learning activities start out being integrated. When it derives from real community needs, those activities are automatically purposeful. They highlight independent and critical thinking, responsibility, communication, collaboration, and problem solving not because someone decided they should be taught but because they are needed to achieve a common purpose.[21]

In his critique of the inert ideas approach to formal education, Whitehead asks, what then should we teach? His answer is a simple one, which emphasizes how putting it all together ought to be the ultimate aim. We should seek to understand the whole frog, and a living one at that: "There is only one subject-matter for education, and that is Life in all its manifestations. Instead of this single unity, we offer children . . . a rapid table of contents which a deity might run over in his mind while he was thinking of creating a world, and has not yet determined how to put it together."[22]

NOTES

1. Jonas A. Banks et al., "Learning in and out of School in Diverse Environments," 2007, 8–9, https://education.uw.edu/sites/default/files/cme/docs/LEARNING%20LIFE%20REPORT.pdf.

2. Kenneth J. Locey and Jay T. Lennon, "Scaling Laws Predict Global Microbial Diversity," *Proceedings of the National Academy of Sciences of the United States of America* 113, no. 21 (May 24, 2016): 5970–75. Estimates such as this offer little comfort when species vital to our own existence are rapidly being driven to extinction.

3. Carolyn M. Malmstrom, "Ecologists Study the Interactions of Organisms and Their Environment," *Nature Education Knowledge* 3, no. 10 (2010).

4. Bill Cope and Mary Kalantzis, eds., *Ubiquitous Learning* (Urbana, IL: University of Illinois Press, 2009).

5. Ann W. Lewin, "Children's Museums: A Structure for Family Learning," *Marriage & Family Review* 13, no. 3–4 (October 12, 1989): 51–73. Children's museums are the best institutional realization of the real stuff idea. The modern incarnation of these started in 1964 with Michael Spock at the Boston Children's Museum.

6. John Martin Rich, "On Educating the Emotions," *Educational Theory* 27, no. 4 (October 1, 1977): 291–96.

7. Gladys Spencer, "Types of Audio-Visual Materials and Equipment to Be Utilized by Libraries in the Educational Program," 1946; Bertram C. Bruce, "Ubiquitous Learning, Ubiquitous Computing, and Lived Experience," in *Ubiquitous Learning*, ed. Bill Cope and Mary Kalantzis (Urbana, IL: University of Illinois Press, 2009), 21–30.

8. Alfred North Whitehead, *The Aims of Education and Other Essays* (New York: Macmillan, 1929), 13.

9. Jane Addams, "Women and Public Housekeeping" (National American Woman Suffrage Association, 1913), 1.

10. Alva Noë, *Out of Our Heads* (New York: Hill & Wang, 2009).

11. Gerry Stahl, *Group Cognition: Computer Support for Building Collaborative Knowledge* (Cambridge, MA: MIT Press, 2006).

12. Debra Hawhee, *Bodily Arts: Rhetoric and Athletics in Ancient Greece* (Austin, TX: University of Texas Press, 2004); see also Richard Shusterman, *Pragmatist Aesthetics: Living Beauty, Rethinking Art* (Lanham, MD: Rowman & Littlefield, 2000).

13. Arthur F. Bentley, "The Human Skin: Philosophy's Last Line of Defense," *Philosophy of Science* 8 (1941): 1.

14. Frederick Matthias Alexander, *The Resurrection of the Body: The Writings of F. Matthias Alexander* (New Hyde Park, NY: University Books, 1969).

15. Lucy Suchman, *Plans and Situated Actions: The Problem of Human-Machine Communication* (New York: Cambridge University Press, 1987).

16. Leo Casey, "Pathways to Competence and Participation in the Digital World" (National University of Ireland, 2009), 155.

17. Alan H. Bond and Les Gasser, eds., *Readings in Distributed Artificial Intelligence* (Amsterdam, The Netherlands: Elsevier, 1988).

18. Edwin Hutchins, *Cognition in the Wild* (Cambridge, MA: MIT Press, 1995).

19. George Lakoff and Mark Johnsen, *Metaphors We Live By* (Chicago: University of Chicago Press, 2003).

20. John M. Carroll, ed., *Learning in Communities: Interdisciplinary Perspectives on Human Centered Information Technology* (New York: Springer, 2009).

21. Bertram C. Bruce, Ann Peterson Bishop, and Nama Raj Budhathoki, eds., *Youth Community Inquiry: New Media for Community and Personal Growth* (New York: Peter Lang, 2014); Ching-Chiu Lin et al., "The Unfinished and Ongoing Business of Art Education in the U.S.: Collaboration, Participation, and Democratic Practices," in *International Handbook of Progressive Education*, ed. Mustafa Yunus Eryaman and Bertram C. Bruce (New York: Peter Lang, 2015), 355–70.

22. Whitehead, *The Aims of Education*, 18–19.

Chapter Five

Networking

> They oppose a schooling process that disrespects them; they oppose not education, but *schooling*. [Many schools] are organized formally and informally in ways that fracture students' cultural and ethnic identities, creating social, linguistic, and cultural divisions among the students in between the students and the staff.
>
> —Angela Valenzuela[1]

The previous chapter shows how learning occurs in diverse guises and places. But the picture is more complex. It makes little sense to discuss an individual organism, such as a termite, as a discrete entity operating in an empty ecosystem. The very organelles within the cells of the termite are built up from symbiosis with bacteria. The protists and bacteria in its gut are operating within a complex network enabling its survival.

Another complex network exists among learners and their niches for learning. In particular, a full view of education cannot be reduced to competition, such as for grades, national test performance, or a race to the top among schools and districts. Interaction among organisms in nature or in learning involves more than simple competition, or even the reproduction and nurturing of offspring.

This chapter focuses on the educational ecosystem in the Paseo Boricua community in Chicago and the Pedro Albizu Campos High School (PACHS), in which the diversity of learning is amplified by the interactions among the activities in the learning spaces. There is a network of connections across formal schooling, after school and community-based activities, political work, social development, and lived experience. Its learning ecosystem is like the lichen, with the network becoming a defining characteristic of the social organism.

Paseo Boricua is admittedly a special case, one which demonstrates a successful approach in difficult circumstances. Even the problems which arise seem to be addressed in positive ways. PACHS supports and benefits a thriving education ecosystem. We should understand it, not as an easily achievable model, but as one end of a spectrum. All of the elements of the ELF—diversity, networking, emergence, construction of learning niches, and interpretation—are evident in the story of PACHS.

Many communities struggle with problems that PACHS has faced—gangs, drug and alcohol abuse, violence, racism, gentrification, homelessness, alienation, poor job prospects, pollution, isolation, and other problems—but with far less success. And most communities are in the big middle ground, with small victories laid against those problems. The lack of communication and shared effort toward a common good makes many of these problems intractable. They especially lack the networking across the ecosystem that stands out in Paseo Boricua.

SOCIAL JUSTICE YOUTH DEVELOPMENT

In her ethnographic account of youth attending a comprehensive, virtually all-Mexican, inner-city high school in Houston (cited above), Angela Valenzuela found that schools actually *subtract* resources from youth by dismissing their definition of education and minimizing their culture and language. Leaders in Paseo Boricua found similar conditions; only one in four of their young people completed high school.

In response to these dysfunctions for students in marginalized communities, Shawn Ginwright and Julio Cammarota propose a *social justice youth development* model. A defining aspect of this model is to help youth develop awareness of their own circumstances as a prerequisite for addressing them. They argue that to promote this praxis of critical consciousness and social action youth need to progress through three stages of awareness.

The first stage, self-awareness, focuses on helping youth achieve a positive sense of self, in terms of social and cultural identity. It encourages them to explore identity issues related to race, class, gender, and sexuality. For the PACHS curriculum, this means learning about the world in a connected way. Literacy follows Paulo Freire's idea of learning to read the word in order to read the world.[2] It means actively participating in that world as both critic and creator. Each student is viewed as a whole, living being; one rarely hears talk of deficits, but rather of caring, strengths, and potentials for growth.[3]

The second stage is social awareness, which fosters an understanding of how their immediate social world functions. It encourages the capacity to think critically about issues in their own communities. The curriculum emphasizes learning how to act responsibly in the world, building on understanding themselves and their Latinx heritage.[4] This ensures that the continuity of lived experiences is a present reality for students, that their daily challenges can be conceived in relation to the larger world and the experiences of others.

The third stage is global awareness, which encourages youth to practice critical reflection in order to empathize with the struggles of oppressed people throughout the world.[5] The curriculum leads to learning how to transform the world, to give back to the community. Classes include video, *bomba y plena*,[6] dance, guitar, and journalism as well as analysis of community resources and challenges. For example, students make podcasts about the history of their school and community. Across disciplines of history, biology, English, mathematics, and others, they learn about themselves as active and responsible participants in civic life.

The PACHS curriculum can be seen as a realization of the social justice youth development model in which self-awareness, social awareness, and global awareness guide growth.[7] Students write and share reflections about work in the community as a way of learning language. They are encouraged to think critically about their learning experiences and to participate actively in their community.

An example of the three levels in practice and in interaction arises in history class. When students are taught about Spanish imperialism in the sixteenth century the ideas may seem very abstract. But if those same students are engaged in a community project to resist gentrification, itself a modern form of colonialism, they understand their self, their social identity, and global dynamics in a more connected way. Applying that awareness in community action furthers their understanding and embodies it.[8]

CONNECTING LEARNING AND COMMUNITY LIFE

Paseo Boricua community leaders advocate for Puerto Rican independence, community resistance against violence, and solidarity with Puerto Ricans and other oppressed people. However, they recognize that young people first of all need a nurturing environment for learning.[9] René Antrop-González quotes a PACHS teacher on this point: "Our students don't come here because they are consciously seeking a liberating education or because they support Puerto Rican independence. They come here because they know that this school will work hard not to neglect them and because they'll find out who they are."[10]

Today, three out of four students complete high school and many have gone on to college. PACHS and the Family Learning Center for young mothers and their children build instruction around students' lives. There are many factors in their success, including dedicated teachers and a curriculum relevant to students' lives. Most of all is the sense of a school community connected to a neighborhood community, with an opportunity to grow in socially meaningful ways.

The success of the program has attracted non–Puerto Rican students. One might predict this would pose a problem in Paseo Boricua, given the emphasis on strengthening Puerto Rican identity and community. But PACHS seems to thrive on diverse interests. It now provides a successful alternative to dominant deficit models employed elsewhere and meets "the affective and cultural needs of the Puerto Rican, Mexican, and African-American students that call it their academic home."[11]

Find Inquiry Problems in Daily Life

Rather than using hypothetical problems constructed from remote situations, possibly long ago, students at PACHS and in similar programs find real, contemporary problems in the community to initiate learning. Examples might include water pollution, racism, economic difficulties, substance abuse, or disputes about building a rail trail. Participation in community life then becomes the hidden resource of the curriculum.

These activities are most effective when they connect learning organizations. Community centers, clubs, museums, libraries, zoos, hospitals, workplaces, online spaces, religious organizations, and other settings, as well as schools and universities, can all be opportunities for learning. When they are connected, their impact amplifies.

In this way, community problems are not just an impediment to education, but a resource that leads to knowledge growth. At PACHS, community members enact this through a variety of organizations, such as the Puerto Rican Cultural Center and the community newspaper, *La Voz*, which plays a central role in a participatory democracy project. There are more formal education elements, such as a day care center, a family learning center, and an alternative high school, as well as a library and community museum. Community action is supported through a healthy lifestyles program, a health center, and Batey Urbano, a club/study center for young people and a venue for social action, where they present poetry with a purpose, hip-hop, and other cultural expressions.[12]

There is also collaborative work to foster development of economic and commercial projects including a Puerto Rican–focused restaurant district. Many of these activities are designed and run by young people in the community and all are conceived as sites for learning for community members of all ages and for visitors.

Urban Agriculture

A large, ongoing project at PACHS is an excellent example of making the outside community become the curriculum. PACHS embodies the community school idea, as well as ideas of transformation and collaborative inquiry, to address community needs. In this case, the "seedbed" that Harry Boyte writes about has a literal meaning as well. Education becomes about transforming both ourselves and our institutions.

The project, Urban Agriculture in the Context of Social Ecology,[13] began as a way for students to learn science through hands-on investigations of hydroponics and soil-based gardening. It expanded to include the study of urban agriculture, community wellness, and economic development.

For example, students grow the ingredients needed for *sofrito*, a sauce used as a base in cooking. These include tomatoes, onions, garlic, green bell peppers, ajíes dulces, oregano, cilantro, and other spices. Growing these and making the sauce contributes to understanding their cultural heritage. Bottling and selling the sauce furthers community economic development as well as affords an understanding of economics and food processing. But the project is not merely about student learning, as important as that is. It is also a central activity of the community, which is seen as a way to address issues of economic development, cultural awareness, and environmental responsibility.

Community as Intellectual Space

Through these projects, the community is seen as a source of knowledge, not simply a place to apply what has been learned.[14] Because it is the arena in which we make sense of the world and ourselves, community becomes the starting point for understanding the sociocultural and natural processes we experience. Thus, community becomes the entrée into the whole curriculum, the map that guides our knowledge and how we obtain it. It also reminds us how education can draw from the problems and the resources of daily life as well as give back to life.

The Paseo Boricua community in Chicago hosted an annual Community as Intellectual Space Symposium for several years. One year, the theme was Critical Pedagogy: Community Building as Curriculum. The conference examined how community building and critical pedagogy can offer effective and sustainable change, locally and among collaborators as well.

There were presentations and workshops on topics such as community-based research, urban agriculture, community informatics, service learning, social emotional learning, critical pedagogy, community health, and community archiving. There were also Batey Urbano's production of Crime against

Humanity, screenings of original documentaries filmed on Paseo Boricua, community tours, and art exhibits.

The concept grew out of discussions among a group of progressive scholars and community leaders. The discussions are meant to cut across disciplines and explore cultural, social, educational, and/or economic intersections of various issues. An underlying aim is to bring people from a variety of occupations and perspectives to address community-wide issues. Researchers need to recognize the capacity of communities to participate in collaborative and critical inquiry toward the issues in their lives.

Learning Spaces and Communities

PACHS is a member of the Alternative Schools Network (ASN) in Chicago, comprising 43 not-for-profit, independent, and self-governing alternative schools, as well as youth and adult education organizations. It serves more than 3,500 Chicago students between the ages of 16 and 21, primarily African American and Latinx. The ASN serves students who are at risk of dropping out, have been previously incarcerated, experienced violence that interrupted their learning, or have disabilities.

Students meet together, typically on a Monday morning, to discuss their school and out-of-school experiences. Typical questions include "Are you learning?" and "If not, why not?" The answer might be that the textbook is boring or seems irrelevant. Students then take on the responsibility of finding a better text, since the goal of learning remains, even if the approach to it is mutable. The classroom becomes an incubator to engage students and teachers as active participants in democratic living, advancing critical dialogue and promoting diversity, equity, and justice.

Schools in the ASN can be described as enacting *La Educación popular* (Popular Education).[15] This bases learning on everyday practices, experiences, and social context. The individual learns from the surrounding environment, not necessarily in formal settings. Paulo Freire's thoughts and work have provided its greatest impetus. The approach is widely used in social justice efforts, including, for example, immigrant rights groups.

La Educación popular proposes that learning comes from the people involved. It cannot be packaged and delivered to be consumed by people who had no say in what it includes. It is often glossed as the practice (or praxis) of freedom. Participants engage with each other as co-learners to reflect critically on the issues in their community and then take action to change them.

Learning grows out of this collective action. Throughout the process, the content of learning is something that the community construes collectively based on its interests and needs. This is psychologizing the subject matter, making it meaningful in the mind of the learner. This is done explicitly by the community of learners, not just by the teacher.[16]

Applying the Ecosystems Learning Framework

An ecosystem curriculum develops systematic ways both to uncover and to contribute to knowledge in the community. This is evident in the many projects within Paseo Boricua. Genuine dialogue enables the community to build on its strengths, rather than to focus on deficits. Self-empowerment for residents develops on the basis of *community funds of knowledge*.[17] Rather than simply transmitting knowledge, education becomes a process of encountering, adopting, applying, shaping, and transforming it.

The ELF could be used to summarize these relations, either for Paseo Boricua as a whole, or for individual projects, such as urban agriculture. It might be quite informative to apply it over time, perhaps starting in 1972, then considering changes each decade and how they enhanced (or hindered) the learning ecosystem.

This thought exercise reminds us that an ELF analysis may be most useful when it explores comparison across situations. Nearly all learning situations have some variety of learning niches; some connections among these often emergent properties are constructed and interpreted to some degree by participants. It becomes more interesting to see how these might change when applied across time or situation.

SUMMARY

Talking about learning at Hull-House, Jane Addams describes college-level lectures and discussions brought into the settlement home. These were valuable, but the residents felt they needed even more to promote a culture to connect people with others. This led to the writing of plays and essays, and teaching by immigrants about their own culture. This is what she calls "socialized education."[18]

It must be noted that the process of connecting community and education or, more generally, enlarging the network for education is not trouble free. It can be challenging to implement anything when everyone is given a voice but not everyone agrees. Importing community values and practices into the educational process means that we are also importing sexism and racism, hierarchy, and limited vision, not to mention simple misconceptions about science and history. And as soon as one community begins to interact with another these challenges amplify.

Nevertheless, community knowledge is vital for democratic education. It also serves an important connection function. In formal learning it is very easy to compartmentalize. The history teacher is not likely to quiz you on how to find the roots of a quadratic equation; the biology teacher will probably not ask you to discuss the UN charter. But when learning starts with life and returns to life it necessarily encounters interactions, connections, conflicts, and other relations among areas of knowledge.

NOTES

1. Angela Valenzuela, *Subtractive Schooling: U.S.-Mexican Youth and the Politics of Caring* (Albany, NY: State University of New York Press, 1999), 5.
2. Paulo Freire, *Pedagogy of the Oppressed* (New York: Continuum, 1970); Paulo Freire and Donald Macedo, *Literacy: Reading the Word and the World* (South Hadley, MA: Bergin & Garvey, 1987).
3. Laura Ruth Johnson, "Challenging 'Best Practices' in Family Literacy and Parent Education Programs: The Development and Enactment of Mothering Knowledge among Puerto Rican and Latina Mothers in Chicago," *Anthropology & Education Quarterly* 40, no. 3 (2009): 257–76.
4. As the school became known for its open and supportive community, it began to attract students from more diverse backgrounds, including African American and LGBTQ students. This led over time to conflicts, and a reevaluation of the school's priorities. The effort to affirm specific cultural identities while becoming more inclusive is ongoing.
5. Shawn Ginwright and Julio Cammarota, "New Terrain in Youth Development: The Promise of a Social Justice Approach," *Social Justice* 29, no. 4 (2002): 82–95.
6. Two different percussion-driven musical traditions.
7. Jeannie Oakes and John Rogers develop similar ideas, showing that engaging K–12 students in community-based research in collaboration with universities can be a powerful mechanism for both education and social change. *Learning Power: Organizing for Education and Justice* (New York: Teachers College Press, 2006).
8. Chaebong Nam, "Exploring Local Civic Citizenship Surrounding the '¡Huntington Park No Se Vende!' Campaign on Paseo Boricua in Chicago," PhD diss., University of Illinois at Urbana–Champaign, 2012, https://www.ideals.illinois.edu/bitstream/handle/2142/30930/Nam_Chaebong.pdf?sequence=1&isAllowed=y.
9. This could be a good example of Nel Noddings's care theory, as in *Caring: A Feminine Approach to Ethics and Moral Education* (Berkeley, CA: University of California Press, 1984); Mark K. Smith, "Nel Noddings: The Ethics of Care and Education," *The Encyclopedia of Informal Education*, January 1, 2004.
10. René Antrop-González, "'This School Is My Sanctuary': The Dr. Pedro Albizu Campos Alternative High School," Julian Samora Research Institute working paper no. 57, June 2003, University of Wisconsin–Milwaukee, 1.
11. René Antrop-González, *Schools as Radical Sanctuaries: Decolonizing Urban Education through the Eyes of Youth of Color* (Charlotte, NC: Information Age Publishing, 2011), 106.
12. Nilda Flores-Gonzalez, Matthew Rodriguez, and Michael Rodriguez-Muniz, "From Hip-Hop to Humanization: Batey Urbana as a Space for Latino Youth Culture and Community Action," in *Beyond Resistance! Youth Activism and Community Change*, ed. Shawn Ginwright, Pedro Noguera, and Julio Cammarota (New York: Routledge, 2006), 175–96.
13. Bertram C. Bruce and Naomi Bloch, "Pragmatism and Community Inquiry: A Case Study of Community-Based Learning," *Education and Culture: The Journal of the John Dewey Society* 29, no. 1 (2013): 27–45; Michelle L. Torrise, "Role of the Library Media Specialist in Greening the Curriculum: A Community-Based Approach to Teaching 21st Century Skills Outside of the School Library through the Practice of Urban Agriculture," *Library Media Connection* 28, no. 4 (February 2010): 18–20; Mihye Won, "Issues in Inquiry-Based Science Education Seen through Dewey's Theory of Inquiry," PhD diss., University of Illinois, 2006.
14. This follows on ideas from Paulo Freire, Ivan Illich, Jean Lave, M. K. Gandhi, and others.
15. *La Educación popular*. Paulo Freire, *Pedagogy of the Oppressed* (New York: Continuum, 1970); Myles Horton, *The Long Haul: An Autobiography* (New York: Teachers College

Press, 1997); Barbara J. Thayer-Bacon, "An Exploration of Myles Horton's Democratic Praxis: Highlander Folk School," *Educational Foundations*, Spring 2004, 5–23.

16. John P. Smith III and Mark Girod, "John Dewey and Psychologizing the Subject-Matter: Big Ideas, Ambitious Teaching, and Teacher Education," *Teaching and Teacher Education* 19, no. 3 (April 1, 2003): 295–307.

17. Norma Gonzalez, Luis C. Moll, and Cathy Amanti, eds., *Funds of Knowledge: Theorizing Practices in Households, Communities, and Classrooms* (New York: Routledge, 2005); Luis C. Moll et al., "Funds of Knowledge for Teaching: Using a Qualitative Approach to Connect Homes and Classrooms," *Theory into Practice* 31, no. 2 (October 1, 1992): 132–41.

18. Jane Addams, "Chapter XVIII: Socialized Education," in *Twenty Years at Hull-House with Autobiographical Notes* (New York: Macmillan, 1912), 427–53.

Chapter Six

Emergent Properties

> The disappearance of tools from our common education is the first step toward a wider ignorance of the world of artifacts we inhabit. . . . Lift the hood on some cars now . . . and the engine appears a bit like the shimmering, featureless obelisks that so enthralled the protohumans in the opening scene of the movie *2001: A Space Odyssey.*
>
> —Matthew B. Crawford[1]

Within an educational ecosystem, there are diverse learning modes, spaces, and purposes, which interact in complex ways. Beyond that, there are properties that emerge from activity within the system.

A simple example of emergence can be seen in the common lichen: It is a composite organism that arises from algae or cyanobacteria living among the filaments of multiple fungi in a symbiotic relationship. The algae or cyanobacteria are protected and anchored by the filaments of the fungi, which also gather moisture and nutrients from the environment. The fungi benefit from the carbohydrates produced by the algae or cyanobacteria via photosynthesis (see Figure 6.1).

Lichens are not plants, or parts of plants, but they can grow on plants, in a further symbiosis. They are also miniature ecosystems, sometimes with additional microorganisms living among the fungi, algae, or cyanobacteria, performing other functions as partners in a system that evolves as an even more complex composite organism. And they are beautiful, as you can see in Haeckel's drawing.

Lichens are among the oldest living things, surviving in an amazingly wide variety of environmental conditions, including extremes such as deserts, arctic tundra, and inside solid rock. They have emergent properties not easily predictable from the components. How can algae and fungi come

Figure 6.1. Lichen as drawn by Ernst Haeckel. *Kunstformen Der Natur, Plate 83: Lichenes*, 1904. Wikimedia Commons.

together to produce fantastic shapes and colors, reflecting properties of their ecosystem?

You may encounter a lichen on a wooden fence rail or along a trail, even in a city playground. Each one is complex, and there are thousands of species. Wolf lichen grows like a leafless mini-shrub, whereas green shield lichen has leaf-like structures. Orange sea lichen grows like an orange crust in open areas on rocks near the sea, but gold dust lichen grows in shaded habitats. Other lichens are powdery, gelatinous, or like matted hair or teased wool. Some lichen grows in isolation, others in colonies.

Lichens come in many colors, and the color changes depending on moisture. Different colored lichens inhabit different sections of a rock face, depending on the angle of exposure to light. They may be spectacular in appearance, such as the vertical "paint" covering rock faces at Yosemite National Park. Added to all of this, lichens interact with other organisms, helping to define the ecosystems of forests, sea dunes, and city streets.

Human organizations also comprise multiple components, which yield emergent properties when they interact. They function like ecosystems in which the elements support, or subvert, each other in surprising ways.

If we could separate the components of a lichen, they would change and die; at the very least, the lichen itself would cease to exist. Similarly, schools need to be linked to other schools and to elements of the society around them. Removing the algae and cyanobacteria from the fungi in a lichen causes it to starve; it withers without a purpose.[2] John Donne's Meditation emphasizes the networked aspect of human life:

> No man is an island entire of itself; every man
> is a piece of the continent, a part of the main;
> if a clod be washed away by the sea, Europe
> is the less, as well as if a promontory were, as
> well as any manner of thy friends or of thine
> own were; any man's death diminishes me,
> because I am involved in mankind.
> And therefore never send to know for whom
> the bell tolls; it tolls for thee.[3]

Conceiving of learning as having at least the complexity of lichen leads us away from the Cartesian view of knowledge as proceeding from one indisputable fact to another. No single individual can be the absolute judge of truth; we must depend on the community. Therefore, we need to "trust the multitude and variety of its arguments." In what could be from a text on rhizomatic learning, Charles Sanders Peirce writes, "Reasoning should not form a chain which is no stronger than its weakest link, but a cable whose fibers may be ever so slender, provided they are sufficiently numerous and intimately connected."[4]

This chapter looks at a variety of examples in various parts of the educational ecosystem. They each show how activity in the world, coupled with reflection, leads to emergent properties of learning. These properties emerge most freely when the various elements of ELF (diversity, networking, construction, and interpretation) are strong.

LEARNING BY DOING

In his *Nicomachean Ethics* Aristotle gives us one of the first statements of learning by doing, as well as of learning from experience. He says that it is through playing the lyre that good and bad lyre players are produced. Similarly, how we act in relation with others determines whether we become just or unjust; our characters emerge from our actions. The acquisition of knowledge, the development of skills, and moral growth all depend upon action in the world.[5]

It is important to understand that for Aristotle this is much more than a recommendation for how to teach. It entails that, to be sure, but it is also about what to teach, and what the ultimate aims of education ought to be. We are not born knowing, nor do we acquire knowledge just by being told. Instead, we grow in virtue by acting in a just way. We are what we do.

Aristotle's statement may seem intuitively obvious, even banal. Of course we learn from experience and from doing things. But its full implications can be surprising: We are not born having a certain character. Nor does our development simply unfold. Nor can it be taught in a didactic way. Instead, it is a result of our participation in the world.

This participation is inherently less predictable than a carefully crafted curriculum that marches through desired skills and bits of knowledge. It is less easy to assess, because we do not know in advance where that participation may lead. Properties of the experience emerge from the situation, just as they do in lived experience.

LEARNING THROUGH COLLABORATING

Although fully grounded in the village of Le Bar-sur-Loup, in southeast France, Célestin Freinet initiated a movement in the 1920s that eventually expanded worldwide: *Pédagogie Freinet,* or the *Mouvement de l'École moderne.*[6] As the movement spread, it began to articulate principles or assumptions, what Freinet calls "*invariants.*" Although Freinet schools spread widely, and have continued as models of innovative pedagogy, they are unfortunately little known in the United States.

Freinet Principles

Freinet lists 30 *"principia de practica educativa"* in one publication, a half dozen of which are shown below. A common theme is that children can learn the most through meaningful work.

- Everyone wants to succeed. Failure is inhibitory, destructive of progress and enthusiasm.[7]
- It is not games that are natural to the child, but work.
- The normal path of [knowledge] acquisition is not observation, explanation and demonstration, the essential process of the School, but experimental trial and error, a natural and universal process.
- The child does not like the work of a herd to which the individual has to fold like a robot. He loves individual work or teamwork in a cooperative community.
- Punishments are always a mistake. They are humiliating for all and never achieve the desired goal. They are at best a last resort.
- The democracy of tomorrow is being prepared by democracy at the School. An authoritarian regime at the School cannot be formative of democratic citizens.[8]

The Freinet school movement grew out of his own experiences as a teacher. During World War I, he had been wounded in the lung, leading, in part, to his becoming a pacifist. After the war, he became an elementary school teacher in Le Bar-sur-Loup, France. Unable to project his voice because of the war injury, he abandoned the traditional lecture approach. He turned the teacher's large lecture platform into a worktable for the students, at which he could guide collaborative learning projects. He then purchased a printing press to produce free texts and class newspapers for his students.

Learning Walks

Soon, the children began to compose their own works, discuss and edit them, and present them as a team effort. Their texts were based on *learning walks*, regular, open-ended field trips into the community to examine the work and social life.[9] Their compositions became newspapers and magazines that could be sent to other schools, such as those in Brittany, in far northwest France.

These interscholastic exchanges became a means to learn about other cultures and languages. Freinet saw that the children's own texts were more engaging and ultimately more educative for the students than textbooks, which held little meaning for their lives.

As the children were experiencing new modes of learning, Freinet worked to support teacher unions not only for better conditions but also for exchange of pedagogical ideas. Teachers would change public education from the inside. He believed that teachers should be intellectuals, social critics, and responsible agents of curriculum and instruction. These theories, added to his socialism, meant that his ideas were rejected in the United States, which emphasized teacher-proof curricula at the time.

For Freinet, practical needs originated and organized experience. Engagement in work provides a basis for examining and constructing our reality. Freinet referred to the activity of his classroom as either the *Modern School*, meaning that it bridges the gap between life and school, or "learning through work."[10] Students learn by making products or providing services.

Based on this practical work, children would learn through inquiry and cooperation. These activities built upon what Freinet called the "natural method." It was authentic learning based on real experiences, with children's interests as the starting point. Both the means and the ends include democratic education: Children, teachers, and parents take responsibility for their work and for the whole community through self-government.

Freinet encouraged children to conduct their own Field Investigations (*sortie-enquête*). This meant that they regularly left the classroom in order to observe and study the local community and the natural environment. In the classroom, they would analyze what they had found, present their results, print out texts, produce a journal, and send it to children in other schools. Teachers also produced magazines such as *The Proletarian Educator* and booklets based on pupils' research projects. These became an alternative to traditional textbooks.

A Larger Movement

Based on school reform in France from the 1920s but expanding after World War II, the *Modern School Movement* is the community of teachers who follow the educational and social practices of Freinet; his wife, Élise; and their successors. The Freinet practices are similar to those of progressive education in the United States, and the Modern School Movement has had a similar international impact. There are related organizations in many countries and affinities with both *Escuela Nueva* and *La Educación popular*.

Freinet's ideas resonate with those of Johann Heinrich Pestalozzi and Friedrich Froebel before him, and Dewey, writing about the same time. But Freinet extends Dewey's ideas of democratic education in several important ways. He shows practical methods for how schools can become sites for democratic living and engagement with the community.

Freinet also talks more explicitly about class, and about issues such as prejudice against immigrants. He then shows ways that schools can address these issues. As evident in magazines such as *The Proletarian Educator*, he recognizes the political dimensions of education and organizes constructive responses to these.

Freinet schools have become a popular form of alternative education in Belgium. A teacher, Anne Van Zwijnsvoorde, says, "Our school is a story about how educators, students and parents become true partners to improve the educational experience for everyone. . . . We do not use traditional punishments."[11] For example, rather than punishing students for (forbidden) walking on the roof of the school, teachers would discuss with the students, and engage them in finding a solution, such as designing better signage.

Freinet's experiences show how properties of learning emerge. A simple walk in the village turns into an opportunity for writing, then a school magazine. The practical challenge of printing the magazine becomes a construction activity with an old, broken printer. Seeking an audience for the magazine leads to communication across regions and languages. Learning for the children becomes learning for teachers, and all is embedded in social and political life.

RECYCLING COMPUTERS

A contemporary example in the spirit of Freinet, combining work, political awareness, and learning, can be seen at a nonprofit organization in Dublin, Ireland. It is named Camara, using the Bantu word for teacher or one who teaches with experience. Some say it is also named for Dom Helder Camara, the Brazilian archbishop, who is famous for saying, "When I give food to the poor, they call me a saint. When I ask why the poor have no food, they call me a communist."[12]

Camara empowers communities in Africa through technology. The project accepts donated computers, primarily from high-tech companies; erases the hard drives; installs open-source software, such as Ubuntu and stand-alone Wikipedia; delivers them to third-world countries; sets up computer centers in schools and libraries; and provides training for teachers, students, and community members. Groups of volunteers train African teachers in basic computer literacy and more specialized technology areas. They also produce computer training materials and educational multimedia in areas such as HIV/AIDS and gender equality.

The Camara network consists of Education Hubs, which are independent local entities responsible for frontline delivery. There are currently hubs in Kenya, Lesotho, Tanzania, Zambia, and Ethiopia, as well as in Ireland. In addition, there are resource centers in Dublin and London. These collect redundant computers from organizations and individuals for refurbishment and reuse. These computers are loaded with educational software before being shipped in bulk, in 20- or 40-foot containers, to the Education Hubs.

Further processing takes place at the hubs before the computers are sent out and set up, typically in e-learning centers in schools.

Several years ago, the National College of Ireland (NCI) had discussions with Camara regarding learning opportunities. It turns out that enacting the Camara model addresses the learning objectives of the NCI third-year work experience requirement, as well as major parts of courses in hardware, multimedia, networks, management technology, marketing, and other areas.

Many students and staff were interested in volunteering with Camara. They can learn from that and at the same time contribute needed expertise. Working with Camara means that the students experience state-of-the-art technology in an environment with real needs, schedules, and collaborators. They see a purpose to their work.

This is an excellent example of the principle: *The community is the curriculum.* When learning grows out of concrete lived experience, learning activities are integrated from the start. When it derives from real community needs those activities are automatically purposeful. They highlight independent and critical thinking, responsibility, communication, collaboration, and problem solving, not because someone decided these should be taught, but because these are needed to achieve a common purpose. All of the participants, including whether in the college, the Camara hub, or a village in Africa, become contributors in a learning community that also addresses concrete daily needs.

As with Freinet's earlier work, Camara shows how the system itself grows. Learning about villages in Africa emerges from what started as simply a way to make better use of discarded computers. The network of connections among Camara, high-tech companies, Dublin communities, African villages, and so on leads to properties not easily predictable from the parts alone.

CHICKEN EGGS AND MRI

Some classroom teachers have used chicken egg incubation as a way to help their students engage more directly with nature. Fertile chicken eggs will usually hatch in 21 days if they are kept warm and not handled roughly. The students can learn about the process of incubation, statistics on hatch rates, growth of the chickens, and more. They can even get a fuzzy glimpse of the embryo developing through a procedure called candling.[13]

Nature and New Technologies

A project called Chickscope expanded on these ideas.[14] Using inquiry-based curriculum materials, interactive Web-based modules on egg mathematics, resources on types of poultry, images of embryo development, and most importantly a learning community for teachers, the project turned what would otherwise be a single classroom hands-on experiment into an ecosystem curriculum.

A key extension was to add access to a remotely controlled magnetic resonance imaging (MRI) instrument. This meant that teachers and students could see the inside of the developing egg in far more detail than they could through candling. Students had to request an image by specifying the orientation of the egg and MRI parameters. The resultant images went into a database that is still accessible via the Web. Students thus acted as researchers, creating scientific data on the Web, not simply finding it or commenting on it.

The value of being researchers rather than consumers of research can be seen in light of a problem that arose with the images. Students were disappointed to find that not all images were clear and definitive, as they might find in a book or website. The parameter settings affected the quality. That quality in turn needed to be defined relative to some purpose. For example, by day six, the beak begins to form. Students might happen upon or search for this and other anatomical features.

Through their trial and error, students discovered experientially that images are not a priori truth, but constructions dependent upon both purpose and technique. But there was a larger problem. Once they learned to construct sharp images, students were dismayed to find sudden, but only occasional, blurred images. This happened after the first week of incubation as the chicks began to move. Just as with a slower film camera, the subject needs to hold still if the photographer is to obtain a clear image. Again, blurry images rarely appear in packaged curricular materials, yet they are an ever-present reality for anyone engaged in original scientific research.

Around day 18 or 19, once blurry images for the embryo sharpened again. This was due to the chick growing to fill the shell. It no longer had room to move. The embryology experts were not surprised by this, but most of the students, teachers, and others involved learned it through confrontation with an anomaly. Working through the anomaly leads to an understanding of the phenomenon. More importantly, it leads to understanding how to proceed when confronting a difficulty. That process is essential to inquiry, not an impediment to it. To the contrary, crisp, packaged images ironically give us a distorted image of the scientific process, that it is about swallowing truths mysteriously accumulated by others.

Piaget describes an anomaly such as those the students found with their MRI as a *disequilibrium*; Vygotsky describes it as entering into the *zone of proximal development*; Dewey calls it a *felt difficulty*. Major learning theories all assert that we learn most when overcoming problems, not by being presented with solutions. Learning how to use and interpret MRI provides those anomalies as part of the phenomena under study and ultimately affords deeper learning.

Learning Community

Through the MRI, simulations, video, discussion boards, and other tools, the World Wide Web became for the students a *World Wide Laboratory*. The scientists involved with running the MRI, analyzing the data, and overseeing the entire project had online forums called "roosts," where they answered student questions. There were also opportunities to use the university's virtual reality theater to "get inside" the developing spinal cord of a chicken embryo.

Perhaps even more significantly, the project helped grow a learning community comprising K–12 teachers, university faculty and students, imaging technicians, farmers, and others. One group of primary teachers developed a collection of children's literature related to eggs and chickens. Some middle school teachers focused on how to weigh chickens and plot growth rate. Another looked at the economics of poultry farming via a simulation. Some of the high school classes emphasized understanding how MRI and other biological imaging technologies work. These activities were shared among the participants and developed further.

Interactions and Emergent Properties

The activities were re-created and co-created by students and teachers. For example, two middle school teachers had students nurture and study the developing chicks. They would weigh them regularly on a small scale. This led to an unexpected problem, one that is not so surprising in retrospect. The chicks would jump around and often off of the scale. Students had to devise a solution. They selected a small cardboard box to hold the chick. But then, of course, they had to subtract the weight of the box from the final value shown for box plus chick.

This revised protocol worked well, but led to another problem: All of the handling by middle school children was stressful for the chicks. Some would defecate, either before or after being placed in the box. Should the recorded weight then include those feces? If not, then should a chick that did not defecate obtain a higher recorded weight?

These practical issues would not arise through study of an online website or a textbook. They arose because of specific exigencies of that classroom, including the particular scale being used and the organization of classroom activities. For instance, multiple weighers might cause greater stress than would one designated weigher. But in addressing particular, situated issues, which did not have textbook solutions, the students had to confront larger questions—the nature of measurement, uncertainty, the quality of evidence, operational definitions, and more. These spoke to the heart of scientific inquiry, much more than would following a preset procedure.

An emergent property of the Chickscope ecosystem was the use of literature. The scientists who initiated the project from the university side focused on imaging as a means of learning about embryology. Teachers welcomed that and learned along with their students. But they also saw ways to connect the science activities with reading. Teachers found nonfiction texts about poultry farming, biomedical imaging, evolution, and other topics appropriate to the curriculum, student interests, and grade level. In the primary grades teachers brought in fiction as well, for example, *Chicken Little*. The work with live animals enhanced interest in reading and the reading in turn informed the science investigations. These properties of the ecosystem emerged through the doing, not as a preplanned package.

Diversity of Learning Activities

The daily "MRI time" is not supported anymore, but teachers continue to use the materials, the website, and the database of MRI. There was a follow-on project called Bugscope, which provided free interactive access to a scanning electron microscope so that students anywhere in the world could explore the microscopic world of insects. Since then, there have been many technological advances, but Chickscope still stands as an example of how one might implement an ecosystem curriculum.

The project illustrates how learning can be enhanced by connecting school, university, farm, and market, and by fostering collaboration among teachers and others. Figure 6.2 shows just a small subset of the learning activities involved. There is dialogue with the teacher, but also with other students, university people, farmers, and others. Students use computers, and via those, the Web, then the MRI instrument. They also use instruments in the classroom, such as a weighing scale, and specialized tools that they build. They interact with the actual eggs and chickens. They branch out into related areas such as egg mathematics, ethics of agriculture, genetics, and more.

One class had discussions about what to do when most of their eggs hatched, but none did in the classroom next door. This led to the development of an "adoption" program, general discussion about fairness and ethics, and dialogue about human adoption. This was clearly an emergent property of a project that began simply to show children the wonders of MRI and embryology.

The indirect experience of nature through videos, webcams, simulations, virtual reality, databases, maps, and other new media, as with Chickscope, can be a wonderful thing. But we also need direct connection with nature.

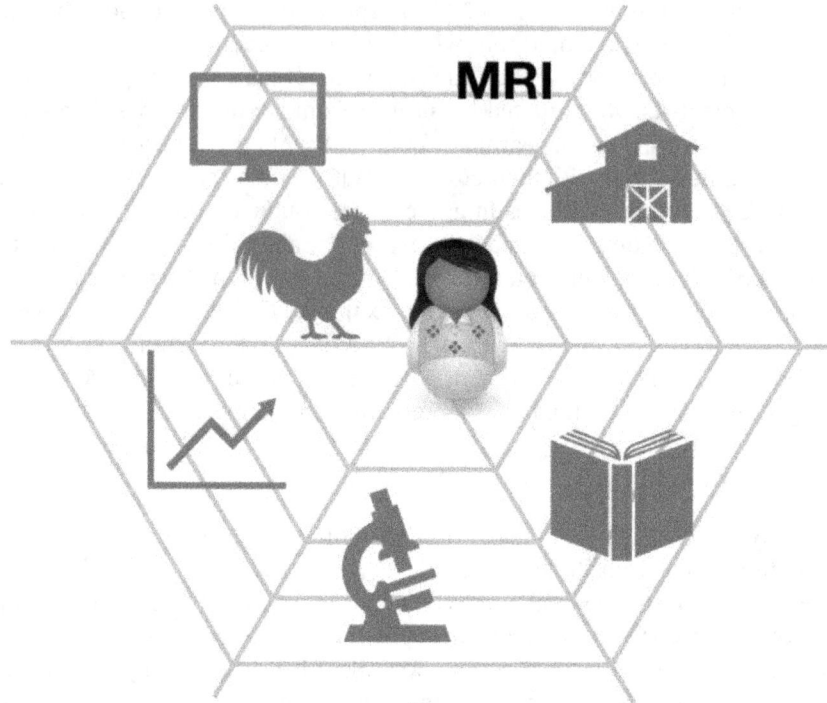

Figure 6.2. Education Ecosystem for the Chickscope Project.

That is why the project saw that raising incubating eggs and raising chickens, or visiting a poultry farm were more important than any online simulation.

Critique through ELF

We can use ELF to view or describe the activities of Chickscope, including its strengths and weaknesses. Table 6.1 suggests a starting point for comparison of the case of studying chickens as one might do in any classroom, the case of that plus using an incubator to hatch chickens, and that plus using MRI to examine images of the developing chick. A study of these could go much deeper, but even a surface analysis reveals several interesting comparison points.

Many of the notes in the table point to positive features. However, each activity always brings negative features as well. One is somewhat ironic. In the effort to teach all about chickens, using multiple media and diverse experiences, the animals became objects of study removed from their ecosystems, whether in a factory poultry production facility, a small organic farm, a free range habitat, or (rarely) in the wild. There was little opportunity to study or talk about these ecosystems. As a result, Chickscope stands as a good example of an education ecosystem but is somewhat lacking as an approach to teach *about* ecosystems, other than the special one that the chicks found themselves inhabiting within a school.

For example, teachers who participated in Chickscope found that the project gave them personal tools to become leaders on other projects in their school or district. Their knowledge of the Internet, MRI, hands-on science in the classroom, relations with the university, and more helped them grow and develop. They also gained credentials respected by parents, colleagues, administrators, and granting agencies. This is noted as an emergent property, something that had not been articulated in the Chickscope design.

Table 6.1. ELF Analysis of Chickscope

Characteristic	Studying Chickens	Plus Incubators	Plus MRI
Diversity	Use of books, video, websites, models, posters	Direct engagement with fertile eggs & live chicks; opportunities for measurement; health & safety issues	New technologies (extra expense, accessible to a few, difficult to sustain), imaging concepts
Networking	Potential to integrate across sources	Connections from models & text descriptions to eggs & chicks; consonance with district's promotion of STEM education	Multiple modalities of exploration; technology emphasis taking away from study of chicken ecosystems
Emergence	Dependent on individual teachers, per classroom	Learning community for teachers; health & ethical issues relating to work with live animals	Benefits for teacher development: new skill set & credentials
Construction	Per classroom	Collaboration in the community on structure of both teacher & student learning; teachers adding literature as an entry point	Shared database of MRI images
Interpretation	Per classroom	Variety of interpretations	Shifting focus from the chicken to imaging modalities

Also, teachers interpreted Chickscope in dramatically different ways reflecting their own experience, their students' needs, the history of the classroom, parental resources, and other factors. One middle school teacher focused on poultry farming economics, an appropriate focal point for an agricultural county. Students created mathematical models, extending their math skills and learning beginning economics along with knowledge of poultry farming. Another emphasized embryology, using the MRI database, university resources such as a professor, labs and AV materials. Two other teachers raised the chickens for a longer time. This led to activities such as growth charts and studies of measurement per se.

As mentioned above, some primary teachers turned to children's literature—stories, poems, and songs about chickens and other barnyard animals. Science questions were still pertinent, but they were situated in a frame that made sense for those teachers and their students. These alternate interpretations are suggested in the last row of Table 6.1, and could also be shown in the row on construction.

Technology promoters from the university interpreted the project as a successful demonstration of the power of new technologies for enabling learning. They were less interested in the details of what children learned, or how some might have been more interested than others in the project. Simply working out (in 1997) how to connect a primary school classroom with the university MRI machine was challenge enough. There were varying interpretations from teachers, parents, science education researchers, university scientists, and others involved.

At its best, Chickscope was just a small innovation, and it came to an end once the funding dried up. It succeeded to the extent it did because it was consonant with the local learning ecosystem, including the value placed on new technologies and university resources, the need for a community of teachers, and the emerging interest in STEM education. One can view that as a recipe for success, but also as a reminder that more radical (dissonant) changes, those that challenge the local ecosystem, are unlikely to succeed.

SUMMARY

In each of the examples presented in this chapter, properties of the learning situation as a whole emerge through actual practice. The work at Camara, for instance, shows how the process of providing computers for Africa must account for power grids, dust, technical ease of use, copyright, cultural and language differences, local health needs, packaging for shipping, multimedia design, and much more. These issues emerge through the doing.

Bits and pieces of these issues may appear in one or another formal course, but rarely do they do so in an integrated or situated way. The emergent properties call for understanding how ideas connect across disciplines and how life activities are only partially captured within formal pedagogical hierarchies.

Whitehead reminds us that "knowledge does not keep any better than fish. You may be dealing with knowledge of the old species, with some old truth; but somehow it must come to the students, as it were, just drawn out of the sea and with the freshness of its immediate importance."[15] There is clearly freshness and engagement in projects like those described here. Moreover, the students undoubtedly learn about design, collaboration, and more, often emergent properties of the work they do, not necessarily predefined curricular goals.

A skeptical reader may well have many questions: Don't these projects have their own ecology? Don't they often start fresh, but later begin to routinize? And all of these uses of "community" refer to the same concept? Is this an efficient way to learn? Does it extend beyond a simple example? What do we say about how it relates to learning through reading, or learning to use complex mathematics? Can community become anything more than a trivial aspect of the curriculum? Can community really be the curriculum?

For many people, notably academicians, learning allows us to rise above our baser instincts, to elevate thinking above feeling, theory above practice, abstraction over concreteness—to create a distance from the body. Many others, perhaps most people, do the opposite, placing "what works" above conceptual frameworks.

Dewey, following Aristotle, rejects this dichotomy, seeing instead that the problems with both intellectual life and the practical world reside in the breakdown of connections between the two, the severing of mind from body. He makes the striking assertion that "the question of integration of mind-body in action is the most practical of all questions we can ask of our civilization."

He contends that by integrating intellectual and spiritual functions with the physical, those functions accomplish something beyond themselves. The integration is not an academic exercise, but a call for action. Accepting neither "soulless and heartless materialism" nor "futile idealism and spiritualism" the integration means that learning is not a prelude to situated action, but a necessary part of it. This justifies hands-on learning or learning by doing within the classroom. But the theory extends learning through life itself.[16]

NOTES

1. Matthew B. Crawford, *Shop Class as Soulcraft: An Inquiry into the Value of Work* (New York: Penguin, 2009), 1.

2. In a similar fashion, the complex and unpredictable forms of a rhizome network inspired Gilles Deleuze and Félix Guattari in their search for a postmodern epistemology. Any point of a rhizome can be connected to any other. Knowledge has no fixed center or position of absolute authority; it evolves based on community needs and perspectives, and it responds to a rapidly changing environment. *A Thousand Plateaus*, trans. Brian Massumi (London and New York: Continuum, 1980).

3. John Donne, *Devotions upon Emergent Occasions* (Ann Arbor, MI: University of Michigan, 1959), 109.

4. Charles Sanders Peirce, "Some Consequences of Four Incapacities," *Journal of Speculative Philosophy* 2 (1868): 140–57.

5. Aristotle. *Nicomachean Ethics*, trans. W. D. Ross (Internet Classics Archives, by Daniel C. Stevenson, Web Atomics, 350AD): Book II, para. 4.

6. Victor Acker, *Célestin Freinet* (Westport, CT: Greenwood, 2000); Isabel Divanna, "The French Educator Celestin Freinet (1896–1966): An Inquiry into How His Ideas Shaped Education," *French History* 22, no. 4 (December 1, 2008): 507–508; Célestin Freinet, *Cooperative Learning and Social Change: Selected Writings of Célestin Freinet*, trans. John Sivell and David Clandfield (Canada: Our Schools/Our Selves, 1995); John Sivell, *Freinet Pedagogy: Theory and Practice* (Lewiston, NY and Queenston, Ont.: E. Mellen, 1994).

7. Here, Freinet means the constructed failure produced, recorded, and reified in schools, not the trial and error of real-world problem solving.

8. Célestin Freinet, *Education through Work: A Model for Child-Centered Learning*, trans. John Sivell (Lewiston, NY: Edwin Mellen Press, 1993).

9. Jan Masschelein presents a contemporary version of this idea in "The Idea of Critical Educational Research: Educating the Gaze and Inviting to Go Walking," in *The Possibility/Impossibility of a New Critical Language in Education*, ed. I. Gur-Ze'ev (Rotterdam, The Netherlands: Sense, 2010).

10. Roberto Otero, "Life and Modernity in L'Ecole Moderne of Celestin Freinet," *Synthesis/Regeneration* 5 (December 1, 1993): 572.

11. Marina Kazakova, "The Growth of the Freinet Movement and Alternative Education in Belgium," *The Word Magazine*, May 5, 2017.

12. Quoted by John Dear, *Peace Behind Bars: A Peacemaking Priest's Journal from Jail* (Lanham, MD: Rowman & Littlefield, 1995), 65.

13. Today, this is more often done by shining a strong flashlight through the egg.

14. The author was directly involved in the project. See Bertram C. Bruce et al., "Chickscope: An Interactive MRI Classroom Curriculum Innovation for K-12," *Computers & Education* 29, no. 2–3 (1997): 73–87.

15. Alfred North Whitehead, *The Aims of Education and Other Essays* (New York: Macmillan, 1929), 98.

16. John Dewey, "Body and Mind," LW 3:30.

Chapter Seven

Finding and Constructing Learning Niches

> People construct community symbolically, making it a resource and repository of meaning, and a referent of their identity.
> —Anthony P. Cohen[1]

Studies of evolution show that organisms do not just inhabit or fit into an ecological niche; they create it. They do this in concert with other organisms. Moreover, even the notion of what the niche *is* or might become is inseparable from the history, needs, and abilities—perceptual, cognitive, and intersocial—of the organism. The physical and biological conditions are interpreted through the life processes of the organism.

Many organisms exist in a diverse array of complex associations; it is the norm. Moreover, those associations occur within biological environments that do not exist independently of the organisms. Richard Lewontin shows that the pertinent features that turn a physical space into a biological environment are often constructed by the organism itself. They do not just find, but create their own ecological niche: "The actual process of evolution seems best captured by the process of construction. Just as there can be no organism without an environment, so there can be no environment without an organism."[2]

This chapter explores various examples of how we continually construct and reconstruct our educational ecosystem. Other elements of the ELF are present as well: Construction occurs most readily within a diverse education ecosystem, which is richly networked and in which properties emerge through practice. Our interpretations of that system guide our actions there.

COMMUNITY

The ecological niche of a tree includes the assemblage of fungi associated with its root system and that of neighboring trees; the shade it imposes on other plants or that they impose on it; habitats for insects, moss, and lichen; chemicals it emits such as the black walnut's juglone; and its attractiveness to beavers, or someone wanting a rope swing, carpenters, or paper mills.

This creative process is amplified in the case of humans. We have a built environment, even if it is only a cleared patch for sleeping in the woods. We have a variety of technologies that we construct, select, and redesign through use. We find and nurture teachers and co-learners. We have books and other media to encode our collective knowledge. There are constructive and collective aspects of our learning niches. Experience does not just happen to us, or within us. It is an active process, which changes the objective conditions for future experiences.[3]

We also construct communities of meaning, which then become crucial defining matrices for our daily interactions. Those communities are very local, as in the neighborhood where we live; global, as in a community of interest online; and extended through time, as in the community of scholars within a discipline.

Community reflects and refracts what we learn and how we apply that. Before that, it is how we interpret experience, describe what we know, or even choose what is worth knowing. This applies not only to social relations, but to specialized scientific knowledge, whose language, questions, methods, standards of proof, and interpretation emerge from community meaning and values. Likewise, community meaning defines both the affordances and the constraints on learning.

For Charles Sanders Peirce, our very reality depends on the combined perspectives of the community, using multiple methods of inquiry. One thought sets the stage for future thoughts. In that sense, a thought today "depends on what is to be hereafter; so that it has only a potential existence, dependent on the future thought of the community."[4] We develop knowledge through a *community of inquiry*. That community becomes a means for learning in the school but also an end, since participation in community enables continuing inquiry and lifelong learning.[5]

HARBOR STUDIES

In the seaside town of Wellfleet, Massachusetts, there is an annual State of Wellfleet Harbor Conference for the entire community. It is held at the elementary school. This is a learning event throughout. The conference explores the complex connections among trout, whales, menhaden, horseshoe crabs, shellfish, sharks, seals, terrapins, sunfish, eelgrass, phragmites, bacteria, protozoa, other living things, the land, sea, and air. Most notably, it considers the interaction of these diverse aspects of nature with people. Every presentation or poster considers ways in which human activity influences and is affected by the rest of nature.

The conference is billed as an opportunity to hear about the latest research. But it is also nature school, or nature as curriculum. Participants, including volunteers, fishermen, students, town officials, and staff of Massachusetts Audubon, the National Park Service, the Center for Coastal Studies, and other organizations, come to report on what they have learned.

The sessions are not simply reports. For example, one session described the history of anadromous brook trout in the area and whether traditional runs could be restored. This was a study of the area, but also an action project to restore the local ecosystem. The research integrated freshwater ecology, the hydrology of Fresh Brook, and history, using archival data from people who lived in the area in the seventeenth and eighteenth centuries.

The presenters asked for listeners to share any family accounts they might have—letters, maps, and so on—which might document the conditions for the trout population from a century or more ago. The listeners, including students and longtime residents, participated in the session, becoming co-investigators in a laboratory for inquiry, not simply a report of results.

The investigation of brook trout thus became collaborative, a community activity, manifesting the Inquiry Cycle (see Figure 7.1). In this case, all members of the community can legitimately *Participate*. Moreover, in each case, participants ask, "What can be done?" Sometimes the answer is to *Create*, which may result in an aesthetic response, political dialogue, collective action for the environment—painting or sculpture, dance, promotion of solar energy, harbor dredging, dam removal, pollution monitoring, and, always, more research. Participants continue then to *Discuss* and to *Reflect* on what they experience, generating new questions to *Ask* along the way. Thus, talk may precede or follow action; reflection may come more with a review of progress or it may be the instigation for new inquiry.

Note that these learning processes overlap. The participation usually demands a lot of healthy discussion. Participants learn as they interact with nature and create solutions to environmental or community problems. Reflection is not something that occurs only in the conference evaluation session, but is an integral part of the talk and action along the way.

The State of Wellfleet Harbor Conference stands out in terms of the collaborative spirit among presenters and audience and in the ways that knowledge creation is integrated with daily experience and action in the world. This learning is not in a school or a university; there are no grades or certificates of completion. There are not even "teachers" or "students" per se. Despite this, one can observe community members finding and constructing

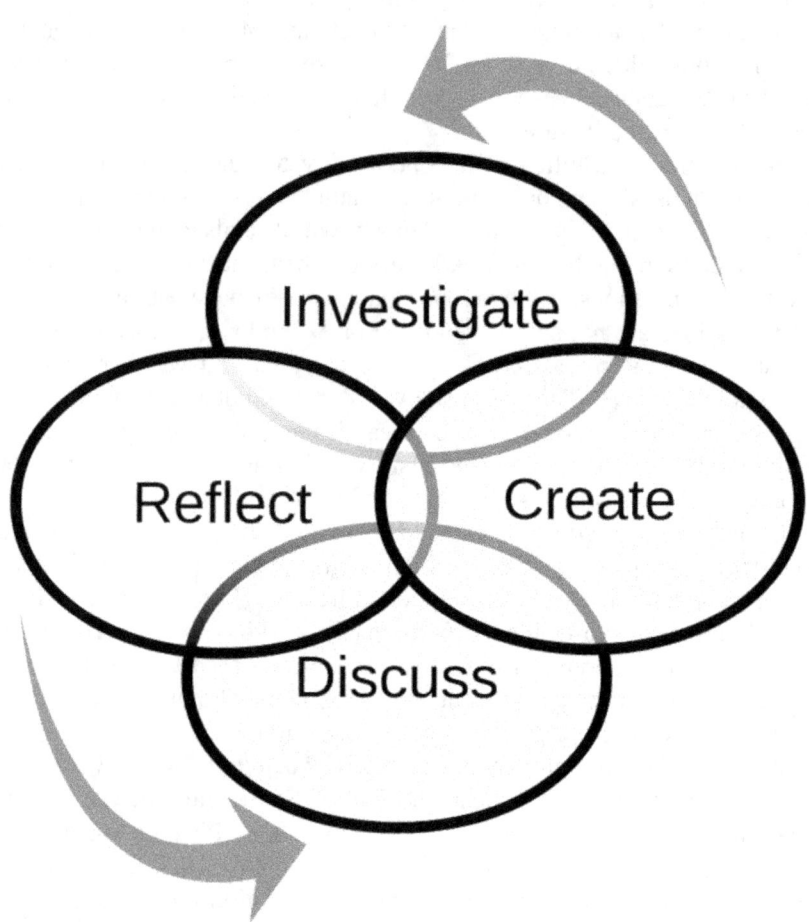

Figure 7.1. The Inquiry Cycle.

a learning niche through disciplines of history, politics, commerce, geology, biology, physics, chemistry, meteorology, and more. Nature itself becomes the curriculum guide.

COMMUNITY-BASED SCHOOLS

The idea of community-based schools was key to the progressive education movement, especially in its later years, as members realized they needed to do more than promote child-centered learning in an individual sense. The community-based school would emphasize youth and community development, family support, health, and human services.[6] It would be created by and owned by the community. A founder of the community schools movement in the United States, Elsie Clapp, writes, "A community school foregoes its separateness. It is influential because it belongs to its people. They share its ideals and its work. It takes from them and gives to them."[7]

Community, and the niches for learning, are thus dynamically constructed by participants. Rather than having a structural definition, it is a cultural field with symbols whose meanings vary among its members. Thus, a community is where we live our lives, but it is also a product of our lived experiences. Despite its centrality to living, community is often disconnected from formal learning.

In a progressive education booklet printed shortly after World War II, "Dare Our Secondary Schools Face the Atomic Age?,"[8] Agnes Benedict describes two visions for schools. In one, the "old school," there is a fence surrounding the building; activities of the school are separate from those of the world around it, and as a result, schooling is separated from the actual life of the children. A second vision shows the "new school." The building is substantially the same, but it is connected to sites for recreation, housing, jobs, health, government, and by implication all aspects of life (see Figure 7.2). The connections are two way, with the school relying on the community as intellectual space and giving back to the community through its processes of study and reflection.[9]

Here, the school connects to home, garden, farm, businesses, and university. Activity centers within the school, such as the kitchen, are linked to corresponding enterprises in the larger community, such as the farm or the grocery market. Neither the academic practices within the school nor the daily work within the community matters more; instead, it is the connection between these that imbues learning with significance.

For children, the activity center responds to their needs for expression, creativity, and social participation. They can bring to school all of their experiences outside of school and then return what they learn to community life. Of course, as anyone knows who has attempted to realize Benedict's second vision, substantive, coherent, working connections between school and community life are difficult to utilize in beneficial ways, even more to develop and maintain.

Clapp contrasts the approach of empowering local people to create community and community schools with the top-down approach that emphasizes simply imparting information about different conditions or gathering statistical data about what exists. Members of the community create changes in their life and learning with other residents based on local funds of knowledge. Her work echoes Abraham Lincoln's phrasing of democracy as government of the people, by the people, for the people.

In the 1930s, Clapp used the planned community of Arthurdale, West Virginia, as an opportunity to create a community school. Students learned

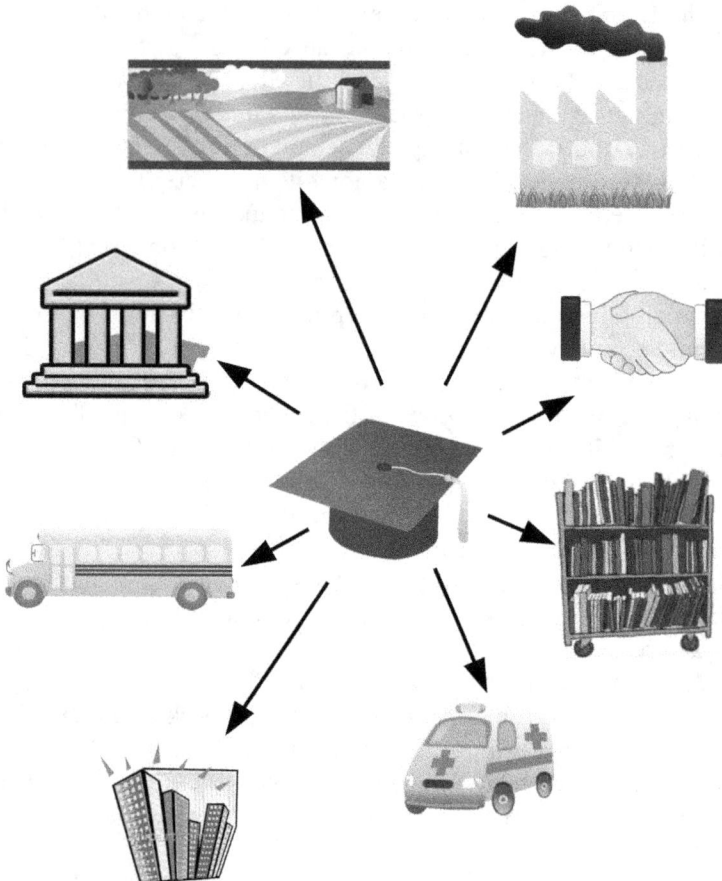

Figure 7.2. The School as Social Center.

about their Appalachian culture and engaged in hands-on projects related to agriculture and construction. This approach built upon ideas of Addams, Dewey, and others that community is the starting point for democracy and ordinary experience is the basis for learning. The school was conceived as a social instrument that valued Appalachian culture, connected it with community, and utilized it to foster identity among both teachers and students.[10]

When the school opened, no school buildings had been built and there were no books and supplies. The teachers improvised and put their progressive teaching plans to work. The second grade learned about construction by watching the workers building homes and put their knowledge to practical use by building their own homestead community. The fourth grade studied pioneer life in an old cabin. High school students combined disciplines and created surveying equipment through their math, science, and shop classes. They surveyed a nearby highway for their final project.

Clapp imagined the school as an experiment in democratic living. It belonged to its people, who shared its ideas and ideals and its work. This meant, for example, that social studies had to be re-envisioned as not only learning about social life, but also participating in it and developing knowledge that could make a difference in that life: A "socially-functioning school" would define its problems as arising from conditions in the community that affected residents, including, of course, the children, and not from hypothetical problems found in a textbook. Members of the school would address these problems and where necessary supply health, social, and recreational agencies to address them.[11]

Rather than simply supplementing schools or being a venue for future activity, the community becomes the intellectual space for learning by all citizens. This societal view applies to community schools per se, but the general principle extends to all schools, urban or rural, large or small, primary or secondary. The school in Yeniceköy, Turkey, pictured in Figure 7.3, is a contemporary example.

The community view also applies to universities[12] and other nonschool sites for learning. Today, many of these ideas have survived under rubrics such as civic engagement, public engagement, community-based learning, or service learning. But often those ideas are seen as one way, going from the university as the seat of knowledge to the masses. They are always limited in scope, for example, as might be applied in a single course.[13]

Working in Alaska in the 1960s and 1970s, Ray Barnhardt saw how essential it was for schools to connect with the communities around them, especially those in rural areas with large Native Alaskan populations. This connection entails changes to the social organization of the school, including changes to the roles of teachers and students. It also leads to new understandings of local culture, and of the very concept of culture per se.

Community-based education calls for redesigning the social organization of the school, in particular to integrate with the cultural patterns of the community. In doing that, teacher and student roles change as well. There is a shared experiential development that can transcend cultural boundaries. In these settings, education for children, job training, adult education, community and economic development, and cultural support merge into a unified community-wide effort.[14]

In the mid-1970s in Colombia, *Escuela Nueva* emerged as a globally recognized innovation that benefits children, teachers, administrators, families, and the community.[15] It was initially aimed at rural multigrade schools where one or two teachers simultaneously teach all grades. Students learn actively, participate, and collaborate, working at their own pace. There is also

Figure 7.3. Community School, Yeniceköy, Turkey.

a focus on the relationship between the school and the community, recapitulating many of Clapp's ideas.

UNESCO's international comparative study showed that, excepting Cuba, Colombia provided the best rural primary education in all of Latin America. Colombia became the only country in which rural schools performed better than schools in urban areas. The World Bank designated it as one of the three most successful innovations that had impacted public policy around the world. *Escuela Nueva* shows the networking that can occur in a successful learning ecosystem and also how teachers and others can construct healthy niches for learning.

We can use the ELF lens to examine any of these community school approaches. Table 7.1 uses the ELF lens to compare Benedict's new school (community based) with the old school (walled off).

Doing so highlights Benedict's vision, but also brings into relief the challenges that impede actualizing that vision. For example, suppose that community work outside the school is primarily dangerous work in mines. It would be challenging to devise a productive way to enhance the school curriculum through that connection. At best, doing so might just reinforce larger inequities when compared to a school which is part of a safe, thriving, diverse ecosystem.

MISIONES PEDAGÓGICAS, SPAIN, 1931–1936

About the time of Clapp's work in the United States, the *Misiones Pedagógicas* began to work in village schools in Spain. Teachers (called "missionaries") delivered literacy programs and cultural artifacts for thousands of adults and children. The project was started by the Second Spanish Republic in 1931 to promote cultural solidarity. It also intended to provide pedagogical support for teachers in rural schools and citizenship education, especially to foster understanding of the democratic principles of the Republic.[16]

A contemporary report tells the story of the *Misiones* through text, photos, and a map. The photos of uplifted, smiling faces may seem overly idealistic today. Nevertheless, it is undeniable that something important was happening for both the villagers and the missionaries.[17]

Led by Manuel Bartolomé Cossío, the *Misiones* included over 500 volunteers from diverse backgrounds: teachers, artists, students, and intellectuals.

Table 7.1. ELF Analysis of Learning with *Misiones Pedagógicas*

Learning Feature	Old School	New School
Diversity	Barrier to outside world; opportunities to learn limited to school activities	Links to all aspects of community life; daunting management problem, safety issues, etc.
Networking	Limited networking; difficulty connecting school learning with community life	Connections to community life across formal & informal learning; community values may be sexist, racist, anti-immigrant, etc.
Emergence	Possible alienation from formal schooling; inert ideas	Stronger conception of the city as a whole; focus on local work arrangements, which may be limiting
Construction	Restricted role for students or teachers to construct learning niches	Community participation in schooling; possible outside school control of controversial topics, e.g., climate change, reproductive rights, social justice
Interpretation	Students making sense of school in their own ways	Otherwise valuable diversity leading to loss of common ground for dialogue and shared work

A former teaching missionary, Carmen Caamaño, said in an interview in 2007, "We were so far removed from their world that it was as if we came from another galaxy, from places that they could not even imagine existed, not to mention how we dressed or what we ate, or how we talked. We were different."[18]

The *Misiones* eventually reached about 7,000 towns and villages. They established 5,522 libraries comprising more than 600,000 books. There were hundreds of performances of theater and choir and exhibitions of paintings through the traveling village museum. Cossío describes the program as follows: "We are a traveling school that wants to go from town to town. But a school where there are no books of registry, where you do not learn in tears, where there will be no one on his knees as formerly" (Figure 7.4).[19]

Teachers would stay in a village for a week at a time. Although the exact program would vary, a typical session might involve showing a gramophone, how it worked, and the construction of the discs. The children would each learn how to make it work. They would then listen to classical and ethnic music, play games, read and discuss romances, and at the end watch films, often shown on a bedsheet screen.

Figure 7.4. Introducing the Gramophone, the *Misiones Pedagógicas* in Navarrisca, 1934. *Patronato de Misiones Pedagógicas*.

The cinematograph (movie projector) often created the greatest astonishment. However, the films were not always fully appreciated. In one instance, villagers watched a U.S. documentary on the production of bread, mentioning the use of lard, which they would never use. So, they just left. Only the young boys and girls kept watching, because they liked the darkness.[20] Incidents such as this reveal how the initial program had to be modified in light of the villagers' preferences and ideas. Villagers and missionaries (teachers) each interpreted the program in their own ways and reconstructed the learning niches.

In her study of Spanish visual culture of the period, Jordana Mendelson examined documentary films and other re-mediations of materials from the *Misiones* experience. Her archival research offers a modern perspective on the cultural politics of that turbulent decade, including the intersections between avant-garde artists and government institutions, rural and urban, fine art and mass culture, politics and art.

In July 1936, a coup sparked the Spanish civil war. Some of the teaching missionaries were killed; many others were imprisoned or exiled. Teachers were accused of instilling a "Republican virus." After the war, the government engaged in "purification" to remove pedagogical innovation, secularism, and coeducation promoted by the *Misiones*. Cossío said, "I don't understand why they hate the *Misiones* so. The *Misiones* wish only to educate. The salvation of Spain will come through education."[21]

One reason for the hate is that when people learn and develop, and especially as they become critical, socially engaged citizens, they inevitably transform their world. They refuse to accept social conditions that had once seemed fixed. The changes that their new knowledge and empowerment engender challenge existing social relationships, conventional practices, hierarchies, and power structures. It is not surprising that Franco saw the *Misiones* as a threat to his power.

Many of the examples in this book show how school experiences can be enriched by connecting to outside-of-school learning, such as for children in the bahal or in Paseo Boricua. However, the *Misiones* are the converse. Villagers were already learning though life; what they lacked were teachers, literacy, formal education, and materials—film, books, phonograph records, and paintings. In both cases, learning practices are less than they might be, due to the ecosystem being restricted.

Spain today is more literate, more urban, more modern.[22] But the economic stress continues for many people. The challenge for achieving social, educational, and economic justice still exists in Spain (as elsewhere), and in some ways seems more intractable.

HELPING CITIZENS PARTICIPATE

A contrasting example is one in which engagement with conditions in the community leads to a focus on learning. In Bucharest, the Resource Centre for Public Participation (CeRe) works for governance closer to the citizens and their needs. Starting with the idea that all politics is local, they help empower citizens and nongovernmental organizations (NGOs) to become involved, mobilize, write petitions, participate at public meetings, contribute to policy making, or even protest in the streets.

CeRe employs an interesting and highly effective community organizing methodology. Although it is based on the specific situations of Bucharest today, its work is a model for community action and community-based learning anywhere.

A relatively small project but one that makes a big difference in people's lives illustrates the process. In an initial phase, community-organizers from CeRe went door to door in the neighborhood to identify problems and possible solutions. They were actively constructing a niche for community improvement, but also for their own learning and that of the residents, in this case with many elder citizens.

One problem they identified was that portions of the neighborhood were separated by a dangerous alleyway, with broken pavement, trash, poor lighting, and unpredictable traffic. Children had to navigate this dangerous path just to attend school. A consensus emerged that repair of the alley was a high priority that appeared amenable to solution. Citizens organized to specify the problem, to propose concrete solutions, and to pressure city officials for action. CeRe advised and facilitated but was not the primary actor.

The goal was to address the immediate problem but, more importantly, to nurture long-term participation in civic processes. Eventually, the alley was cleaned and paved. The city installed bollards to prevent traffic, lighting to improve safety, and trash bins to reduce litter. It is now a safe route between sections of the neighborhood, and even a safe playground.

One could describe CeRe's projects as empowering citizens to speak truth to power. But as Noam Chomsky says, this can be a waste of time; power does not listen. He argues to speak truth to young people instead, since they are the ones who can change the world.[23] CeRe shows that the concept of "young people" needs to include people of any age who are willing to learn and collaborate for the common good.

Other civic renewal projects facilitated by CeRe include turning vacant land into a park and renovating an old movie theater to become a community center. CeRe operates on the assumption that democratic living requires far more than a parliamentary government: It entails free and fair elections, but also a political environment in which citizens can actively participate in the decision-making process.

The staff recognize that this active participation cannot occur without learning; teaching has become a central aspect of what it does. The process is nonlinear and often requires stepping back, moving sideways, or redirecting energies to achieve the goals. Along the way, citizens learn not only about the specific problem but also about working together, listening to each other, making decisions together, being a team, compromising, negotiating, discussing issues productively, and understanding the laws and municipal government.

CeRe works to achieve democratic ends by democratic means, within the context of a progressive education ethos. The process is captured well by Alexander Livingston (speaking more generally on democratic theory): "Political action under conditions of uncertainty is a process of experimentation. It is a creative adventure into the unknown that transforms self, world, and values."[24]

CeRe operates in a context of repressive public policies. In June 2019, the Romanian Senate legal committee promoted an initiative to restrict the civic action space. Among other things, it provides for dissolution of any NGO when it pursues a purpose other than that for which it was established. Initiatives such as this limit the civic groups' ability to communicate with public authorities and weaken its capacity to represent communities' interests. It is an unfortunate example of how the larger ecosystem can hinder as well as help education.

LEARNING ONLINE

Ivan Illich used the term *educational web* long before its use today to refer to the online version, but in essence his characterization is still a propos: "The current search for new educational funnels must be reversed into the search for their institutional inverse: educational webs which heighten the opportunity for each one to transform each moment of his living into one of learning, sharing, and caring."[25]

The evolution of information and communication technologies (ICTs) offers a parallel to the general argument in this book, especially regarding finding and constructing ecological niches. Early proponents for ICTs in education saw the computer as an eventual replacement for teachers or, at least, as a tutor for isolated skills. Integration of those skills into larger contexts, critical engagement, and applications might be left to a human teacher. That approach continues and, indeed, is useful in specific contexts, but it has been supplanted to a large extent by the construal of the computer as a tool.

The PLATO system was an archetype of early computer-assisted instruction. It started at the University of Illinois in 1960. By the early 1970s it had evolved into the nexus of an active user community which re-created it. From 1973 to 1974, PLATO's high school and college students created online message forums, chat rooms, graphical multiplayer games, instant messaging, email, and primitive emojis. They were appropriating the technology, using it for their own purposes far beyond what the designers had envisaged, and re-creating the toolbox to serve their needs.[26]

The computer toolbox then becomes an educational resource constrained only by our imagination (Figure 7.5). It aids our *participation* in daily life, in work, and with nature. It broadens our *communication* network. It may enhance communication with a teacher and with other students. It also takes us beyond the classroom to link with others in the community, the workplace, and around the world, using text, images, maps, music, video, simulations, databases, and virtual and augmented reality.

As such the computer and Internet become aids to finding and constructing learning communities. They are tools for creation and transformation, including the production of new forms of scholarship, technology, and aesthetics.[27] Communities are created and extended through the online world. Cognition is distributed across multiple thinking agents, essentially becoming group cognition. A consequence is that users construct ever larger learning niches. Whereas the traditional classroom may be viewed as having well designed, but small niches, the online world becomes unruly learning in the wild.[28]

In the virtual space, we reinvent the physical world in ways that replicate, reinforce, or undermine its functions depending on the circumstance.[29] The online interactions also lead to new ways of creating and using knowledge. Individuals transfer and exchange tacit knowledge through observation and imitation. Through dialogue and inquiry they convert tacit knowledge into explicit knowledge, or create knowledge through a combination of existing concepts. Processes such as these are enhanced and made visible through online tools.[30] Students respond to different media in individual ways, but all learn best from a suitable combination of media.[31]

Young people today experience the world in new ways through digital media, including mobile devices and the Internet.[32] These experiences are often liberating and integral to the development of identity and social relations, but they can also be excessively individualized, aimless, isolating, and coercive.[33]

Among the new media are open educational resources. These are teaching, learning, and research resources that can be used freely and repurposed by others. They include various tools, materials, and techniques to support access to knowledge, such as course materials, textbooks, videos, tests, simulation software, protein and DNA databases, Wikipedia, and more. Technology-enhanced clubhouses, museum and library programs, science camps, and

Finding and Constructing Learning Niches

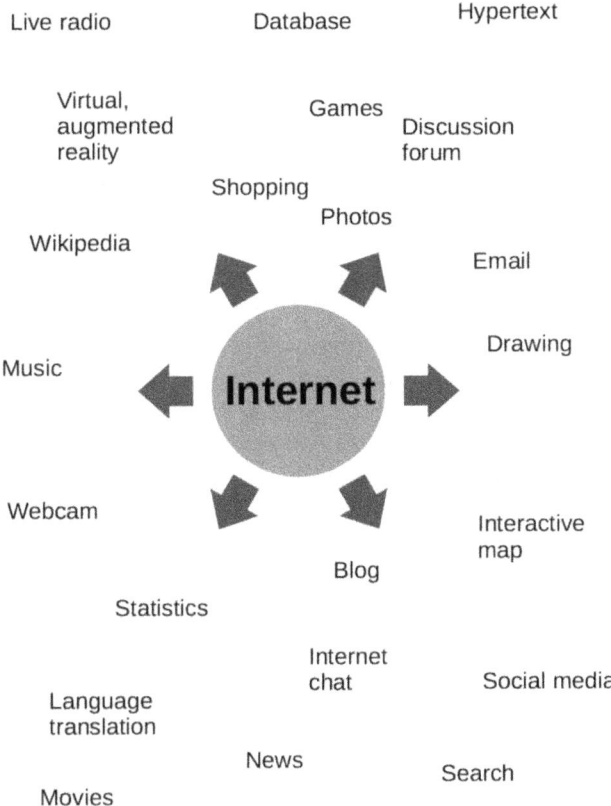

Figure 7.5. The Internet and New Media.

other forms of informal learning play an increasing role in supporting inquiry and community learning.[34]

Young people also use writing in new media to promote active citizenship and participatory action research.[35] A project such as Youth Community Inquiry (YCI)[36] shows how youth energy and facility with new media can address community needs in a concerted way. It also shows how online activity can be integrated with ordinary community life, with collaboration among diverse learning spaces, including urban and rural communities, schools, public libraries, community centers, a public media station, 4-H, and universities.

The use of new technology goes beyond social media, per se, to include building geographic information systems, designing community technology centers, hosting Internet radio and podcasts, video production, and the use of archives and databases. It brings in the perspective of community members in the selection of problems, design of activities, and the interpretation of results. Outside-of-school learning thus helps young people build stronger ties with their own communities, by using new media to help the communities thrive.

For example, in one city in Illinois, African American youth used community asset mapping to identify potential resources of their neighborhood. This included doing oral history and producing databases, videos, and formal presentations to record their findings. They learned that there had been a robust jazz tradition in their community. They interviewed older musicians to hear stories about that and to hear their music. In turn, they shared their own music with the older musicians.

Fluency with diverse digital media can facilitate social change, through mapping community assets, writing community history, and other projects. Young people can build upon their actual or latent abilities with digital photography, audio and video production and editing, Internet search, GPS, databases, Internet radio, and more. This means that they use their facility with new information tools in a way that helps connect and build community rather than leading to further isolation. Digital literacy then becomes not just another skill to acquire but a part of one's repertoire for meaningful action in the world.

Using technology in this way means that learners become active, critical users rather than passive recipients of technology. Their devices become part of their social practices. The online activities are networked with other aspects of life, leading to emergent properties, such as a growing interest in community history. This learning system is constructed by the participants, with cultural, political, and economic values embedded. Users gain agency as they adapt technical systems to achieve personal and community goals.[37]

SUMMARY

The bahal example from chapter 4 should remind us that learning occurs in all sorts of ways through daily life. Even there, that learning did not just happen; the conditions for it were shaped by the actions of the bahal residents. This chapter goes even further in emphasizing how we construct communities, organizations, projects, technologies, and other intentional learning niches.

The belief that thinking globally but acting locally is a viable strategy is a hope more than an established fact. However, these examples do demonstrate that local action can lead to substantial change within communities, that individuals learn and grow from their involvement, and that they can construct new niches for learning. They teach us what civic involvement looks like and provide a vision for the development of civic intelligence.

NOTES

1. Anthony P. Cohen, *The Symbolic Construction of Community* (New York: Routledge, 1985), 118.
2. Richard C. Lewontin, *The Triple Helix: Gene, Organism, and Environment* (Cambridge, MA: Harvard University Press, 2000), 48.
3. Related ideas are developed by John Dewey in "Experience and Education," LW 13:22, and Hans Joas, *The Creativity of Action* (Chicago: University of Chicago Press, 1996).
4. Charles Sanders Peirce, "Some Consequences of Four Incapacities," *Journal of Speculative Philosophy* 2 (September 14, 1868): 157.
5. Charles Sanders Peirce, "The Fixation of Belief," *Popular Science Monthly*, November 1, 1877.
6. See implications for social studies education today in Sarah E. Montgomery, "Re-envisioning Social Studies with the Community School Model of Elsie Ripley Clapp," *Social Studies Research and Practice* 9, no. 1, Spring 2014. Also, Sam F. Stack, *Elsie Ripley Clapp (1879–1965): Her Life and the Community School* (New York: Peter Lang, 2004).
7. Elsie Ripley Clapp, "A Rural Community School in Kentucky," *Progressive Education* 10 (1933): 128.
8. Agnes E. Benedict, "Dare Our Secondary Schools Face the Atomic Age?" (New York: Hinds, Hayden and Eldredge, 1947).
9. Similar diagrams appear in John Dewey's "The School and Society," MW 1:49.
10. Elsie Ripley Clapp, *Community Schools in Action* (New York: Viking, 1939).
11. Elsie Ripley Clapp, "The Teacher in Social Education," *Progressive Education* 10 (1933): 286–87.
12. Lee Benson, John Puckett, and Ira Harkavy, *Dewey's Dream: Universities and Democracies in an Age of Education Reform* (Philadelphia: Temple University Press, 2007).
13. Ann Peterson Bishop, Bertram C. Bruce, and Sunny Jeong, "Beyond Service Learning: Toward Community Schools and Reflective Community Learners," in *Service Learning: Linking Library Education and Practice*, ed. Loriene Roy, Kelly Jensen, and Alex Hershey Meyers (Chicago: American Library Association, 2009), 16–31.
14. Ray Barnhardt, *Culture, Community and the Curriculum* (University of Alaska Fairbanks: Center for Cross Cultural Studies, 1981), para. 90.
15. Vicky Colbert, Beryl Levinger, and Óscar Mogollón designed the model, which is now used in many countries. "Historia de La Fundación Escuela Nueva," *Fundación Escuela Nueva*, n.d., http://escuelanueva.org/portal1/es/quienes-somos/historia-fundacion.html.
16. Francisco Canes Garrido, "Las Misiones Pedagógicas: Educación y Tiempo Libre en La Segunda República," *Revista Complutense de Educación* 4, no. 1 (1993): 147–68.
17. From today's perspective, the project has overtones of imposing dominant culture on rural residents, but it needs to be understood in the light of the Second Republic's democracy agenda, the lack of access to education, and the effort to recognize the capacity of people in the villages to learn and participate in civic life. See more in Patronato de Misiones Pedagógicas, *Patronato de Misiones Pedagógicas: Septiembre de 1931–Diciembre de 1933* (Madrid: S. Aguirre, 2009); Iván M. Jorrin Abellán, Sara Vilagrá Sobrino, and Sara García Sastre, "The Rural-Urban Paradox in Primary Schools: 140 Years of Progressive Education in Spain," in *International Handbook of Progressive Education*, ed. Mustafa Yunus Eryaman and Bertram C. Bruce (New York: Peter Lang, 2015), 571–85.
18. Christian Roith, "High Culture for the Underprivileged: The Educational Missions in the Spanish Second Republic 1931–1936," in *Erziehung Und Bildung in Ländlichen Regionen–Rural Education*, ed. Claudia Gerdenitsch (Frankfurt am Main: Peter Lang, 2011).
19. Manuel Bartolomé Cossio, 1931, quoted in Nigel Dennis, "Ramón Gaya y El Museo Del Pueblo de Las Misiones Pedagógicas," *Escritura e Imagen* 7 (2011): 15–26.
20. Roith, "High Culture for the Underprivileged," 179–200.
21. No comprendo por qué odian de esa manera a las Misiones. Las Misiones no hacen más que educar. Y a España la salvación ha de venirle por la educación. Manuel Bartolomé Cossio, 1934, quoted in Eugenio Otero Urtaza, *Manuel Bartolomé Cossío: Trayectoria Vital de Un Educador* (Madrid, Spain: CSIC y Amigos de la Residencia de Estudiantes, 1994), 386.

22. Jordana Mendelson, *Documenting Spain: Artists, Exhibition Culture, and the Modern Nation, 1929–1939* (University Park, PA: Penn State University Press, 2005).

23. Noam Chomsky, *Chomsky on Mis-Education* (Lanham, MD: Rowman & Littlefield, 2004), 21.

24. Alexander Livingston, "Between Means and Ends: Reconstructing Coercion in Dewey's Democratic Theory," *American Political Science Review* 111, no. 3 (2017): 522–34, para. 4.

25. Ivan Illich, *Deschooling Society* (New York: Harper & Row, 1971), v.

26. Brian Dear, *The Friendly Orange Glow: The Untold Story of the Rise of Cyberculture* (New York: Penguin Random House, 2018); Ron Eglash et al., eds., *Appropriating Technology: Vernacular Science and Social Power* (Minneapolis, MN: University of Minnesota Press, 2004).

27. Robert Taylor calls this third mode *tutee* in his early collection, *The Computer in the School: Tutor, Tool, Tutee* (New York: Teachers College Press, 1980).

28. Caroline Haythornthwaite and colleagues have studied this wild through online sites such as Reddit and Q&A forums. These sites such represent a growing portion of learning for many people. There is a potential to support self-motivated learners and to sustain communities of practice, but more fundamentally extend learning across time and space, and across multiple learning agents. The theory is developed in "Rethinking Learning Spaces: Networks, Structures and Possibilities for Learning in the 21st Century," *Communication, Research and Practice* 1, no. 4 (2015): 292–306; empirical work support can be found in Caroline Haythornthwaite et al., "Learning in the Wild: Coding for Learning and Practice on Reddit," *Learning, Media and Technology* 43, no. 3 (2018): 219–35.

29. Caroline Haythornthwaite et al., "Community Development among Distance Learners: Temporal and Technological Dimensions," *Journal of Computer-Mediated Communication* 6, no. 1 (September 2000), Abstract.

30. Boris Otto and Hubert Osterle, "Principles for Knowledge Creation in Collaborative Design Science Research," Thirty-Third International Conference on Information Systems, Orlando, FL, 2012.

31. Bertram C. Bruce, Heather Dowd, Darin M. Eastburn, and Cleora J. D'Arcy, "Plants, Pathogens, and People: Extending the Classroom to the Web," *Teachers College Record*, April 1, 2017, 1–36.

32. Julie Coiro et al., *Handbook of Research on New Literacies* (New York: Routledge, 2014).

33. Tina Besley and Michael A. Peters, *Re-Imagining the Creative University for the 21st Century* (Rotterdam, The Netherlands: Sense, 2013).

34. Yasmin B. Kafai, Kylie A. Peppler, and Robbin N. Chapman, *The Computer Clubhouse: Constructionism and Creativity in Youth Communities* (New York: Teachers College Press, 2009).

35. See, for example, publications in The Kinder & Braver World Project Research Series (Danah Boyd and John Palfrey, editors).

36. Bertram C. Bruce, Ann Peterson Bishop, and Nama Raj Budhathoki, eds., *Youth Community Inquiry: New Media for Community and Personal Growth* (New York: Peter Lang, 2014).

37. Martin Wolske, "Demystifying Technology: Community Inquiry for Social Change and Transformative Action," 1–13, Monash Centre, Prato, Italy, 2014.

Chapter Eight

Interpretation of Learning Spaces

> The correct analogy for the mind is not a vessel that needs filling, but wood that needs igniting—no more—and then it motivates one towards originality and instils the desire for truth.
>
> —Plutarch[1]

What counts as significant in an environment cannot be disentangled from the needs and activities of the organism. For cold-blooded animals, the ambient temperature is more salient than it is for warm-blooded ones because the latter can more easily regulate their internal temperature. Birds and insects can see colors that are invisible to us. Different organisms evolve their unique characteristics to take advantage of environmental factors like tidal forces, magnetic fields, and other aspects of the physical environment. Different species have their own social environments, including culture and learning, which are opaque to other organisms.

Relative significance is even more salient for humans. For both babies in strollers and people in wheelchairs the availability of an elevator, or a smooth sidewalk, matters more than for someone more ambulatory. Moreover, humans make sense of their environments, acting based on their interpretation, which may be radically different depending on their beliefs, values, and experiences. To say that education is for career, or citizenship, or enlightenment does not mean much until we can say what those terms mean. We must accept that their meaning has shifted across regions, time periods, and simply according to individual values.

People learn and thrive through their educational ecosystem. They learn both by listening to others and by sharpening and deepening their own ideas as they articulate them. Throughout, they interpret their experience and make personal meaning. This chapter continues the discussion of ELF (diversity, interaction, emergence, construction, interpretation) as it examines how one learner interpreted her own learning spaces, developing her own identity as she made sense of that learning.

VESSEL OR FIRE?

Plutarch has some remarkably modern observations on learning. His idea that education is not about filling a vessel but igniting a fire foreshadows Paulo Freire's distinction between banking and problem-posing education. In this metaphor, the vessel model is most commonly associated with lecturing, or the chalk-and-talk style of teaching. But it often undergirds nominally student-centered approaches, too. This could happen, for example, when a hands-on activity is chosen because it promises to be a more engaging way of leading students to a preselected correct idea, rather than as a way to open up the process of learning.

Interestingly, most people who employ the vessel/fire metaphor take it to be a guide for the teacher. They might say, "Do not think of transferring facts, but of inspiring your students." But Plutarch is speaking directly to the learner. He encourages students to grasp the basic points, or what he calls the "seed." He thus admits the need for a balance between taking in predigested basic points and original thinking. A learner needs to combine listening with originality, all toward the aim of living a good life. Ongoing dialogue with a teacher and others can keep that fire going and expand it into new areas.

WEBS OF SIGNIFICANCE

In an effort to understand the impact of a cultural gallery of the Indianapolis Children's Museum, Jean Umiker-Sebeok found that the diverse needs of different visitors led to entirely different experiences. Visitors would construct meaningful spaces in which to move and maneuver to their own advantage. Although in nominally the same exhibit, their reality was of dramatically different exhibits, leading to different experiences and different learning.[2]

Some visitors were classified as relying predominantly on a pragmatic reception strategy, which meant the efficient accumulation of new information. For them, the gallery was a workshop for the acquisition of discrete skills or ideas. Others, manifesting the critical strategy, favored the acquisition of ideas, valued for their place in an abstract order, whether or not this proves "useful" in any concrete way. They sought to assimilate the order imposed by the curator, rather than finding a personal meaning, and were, not surprisingly, the curator's favorite visitor type.

The utopian strategy emphasizes imaginative self-exploration. The gallery visit becomes an act of self-expression, including the exploration of social relationships with co-visitors or staff. Finally, the diversionary strategy stresses the nonutilitarian values of the gallery as an amusement park. Sheer enjoyment is the desired optimal experience. Umiker-Sebeok says this strategy is most antithetical to that of the curators, but characterizes the largest group of visitors in her study. One could see similar dynamics operating in the bahal life, discussed in chapter 4.

Without a detailed study such as this one it can be difficult to see how different the experiences of visitors might be, or by extension, how different students on the same class roll inhabit different classrooms. Clifford Geertz writes that "man is an animal suspended in webs of significance he himself has spun."[3] We cannot extricate ourselves from that web of significance, only seek to understand it and our place within it, perhaps to spin it more beautifully. Learning must be understood in terms of those webs.

There is a complex web of factors shaping learning, including the learner's own interests, attitudes, values, and beliefs. Within that web one learner may benefit from approaches that fail for another, or even for the same learner at a different time. A specific teacher, whether one formally designated as such, or a family member or friend can mean more than a formal curriculum or materials. We construct our own learning ecosystem and interpret it in light of our own web of significance.

Moreover, we are not passive recipients of a curriculum, but active agents who build the curriculum in collaboration with teachers, other students, and people beyond the classroom. We also interpret present experiences in light of our past experiences, attitudes, beliefs, and values.

EDUCATION BIOGRAPHIES

An examination of education biographies, or simple reflection on one's own learning, shows how important webs of significance can be, as well as highlights the limitations of the vessel-filling model for learning. When asked to reflect on their education, most people are unable to recall much of the specific academic content, whether that be the proper use of a gerund or how to find the roots of a quadratic equation. They would perform poorly on the same course final exam that they had mastered just a few years earlier. At the same time, they recall significant experiences, even epiphanies, which shaped their lives. Typically, these did not occur in a classroom.

One of the best known of such reflections is in Henry Adams's ironically titled autobiography, *The Education of Henry Adams*. He tells of his struggle to understand the twentieth century, and how poorly he was prepared to do so by his formal education. Written in third person, Adams complains about the irrelevance of his schooling: "Nothing in education is so astonishing as the amount of ignorance it accumulates in the form of inert facts."[4]

Most people are like Adams. When asked to recount significant learning in their lives, they focus more on experiential learning and informal education. Even when they identify a memorable event in school it tends to be extracurricular, such as time with the math teacher who would come in an hour before the start of the regular school day to introduce students to computer programming or the English teacher who spent extra time discussing the feelings conveyed in a poem by Anne Sexton.

Educational biographies reveal much about the individual learner and can be useful as a guide for that person's further learning. But even a cursory review of any one biography tells us much about how we all learn. Though it may at first seem idiosyncratic, inconsistent, and contingent, delving into the details can be a powerful means to understand the systemic interconnectedness of learning.[5]

In this chapter, we look in detail at one learner in order to see how the education system operates, and in particular, how formal schooling relates to the overall environment for learning. Through various episodes in that learner's path, a complex ecosystem of learning operates, including elements both in and out of school, and in the relations between these, as well as the influences of both prior experiences and evolving beliefs and values. Each episode relates to some kind of formal instruction, although the versions of those are dramatically different.

UNDERNOURISHED SCHOOL

Let us consider the winding path one woman took, learning through school, through out-of-school learning activities, and through experiences in daily life. Ati's experiences display in a striking way aspects of the functioning of the entire ecosystem of education. Each school she attended represents an alternative mode of learning community. Moreover, each is linked with the surrounding ecosystem in notable ways. Ati has a fascinating life/learning journey, which intertwines with several significant educational enterprises of the last century. Her interpretation of these learning experiences led to her co-creation of her own learning niche.[6]

Ati's story is far from typical in its specific episodes; few people experience the same immersion in major intellectual communities, material privilege, or hardships, including the early death of her mother and the rise of the Nazis. Yet it also stands as an archetype of the diverse ways that we all learn.[7]

Beate (Ati) Gropius Johansen was born in Wiesbaden, Germany in 1926, during the time of the Weimar Republic (1919–1933). There was a new democratic constitution, which included proportional representation and voting rights for women. The Republic was the backdrop of hopes for positive social change and creativity leading to a new, modern Germany. But there was also widespread bitterness over the World War I settlement, crushing unemployment, political disturbances, and social unrest.

Ati's early formal education was in a rigid, competitive, and hierarchical environment. Scholastic performance was what mattered. German schools of the time emphasized social hierarchy and obedience to authority, norms that clashed with the idealism of the Weimar Republic, but accorded well with the Nazi regime on the horizon. She was initiated into an early formal education that could be described as undernourished.

There was little opportunity for arts or creative expression. Learning was nearly all text-based, rarely involving hands-on activities or projects. There was no effort at building a learning community within the school or for connecting the life of the school to the larger world beyond. Ati remembered it vividly, but she appeared to have interpreted it as an experience to be endured, rather than as one to guide her life. On the other hand, she developed a respect for excellence and a capacity for detail that may be attributable to that time.

COMMUNITY NEGATING LIFE

After Hitler assumed power in 1933, everything changed. Teachers had to swear an oath of allegiance to Hitler and teach in accordance with ideas and values from National Socialism. They had to join the Nazi Party. Many would come to teach dressed in a Nazi uniform. All Jewish teachers were dismissed. A new course of study was introduced called *Rassenkunde* (race knowledge). At the entrance to the school building, students had to lift their arms and say, "Heil Hitler!"

It is important to note here that the linkage of German schooling to the National Socialism program is a good, albeit horrific, example of education's ecosystem in operation. The Nazis' idea of community became the curriculum in a destructive way. Thus, otherwise appealing ideas such as connecting classroom learning to life beyond school, or that the community should be the curriculum, need to be understood as having negative as well as positive potential.

Ati had a brief experience of Nazi education to add to her biography. Although she never referred to either that experience or the earlier rigid and hierarchical traditional schooling as meaningful for her life, they obviously affected her. The distaste for politics that she expressed later may have been born in those early years.

COMMUNITY AFFIRMING LIFE

The Gropius family managed to flee Nazi Germany in 1934, using the pretext of attending a film propaganda festival in Italy. From there they went to Britain, where they lived for three years. Ati enrolled in the Beacon Hill School, founded by Dora and Bertrand Russell, and directed by Dora.

Ati says about her first encounter with the Beacon Hill School: "In a green garden, surrounded by rolling green fields, lay a large English manor house with French doors wide open to the spring sun. Shrinking and giggling half naked children raced randomly over the lawns paying no attention to our presence, or that of any adults." That moment must have been surreal after her school experiences in Berlin. Indeed, much of the meaning of Beacon Hill for Ati was in the contrast it provided to her early educational experiences in Germany: "There appeared to be no discernible discipline in order of any kind, and I knew instantly that I loved the place. Beacon Hill was a child's garden of earthly delights."[8]

The environment had been created as an intentional counter to the traditional British schooling of the day, which must have been similar to that which Ati found in her first school in Berlin. In the 1927 prospectus, the Russells asserted

> that no knowledge of any sort or kind should be withheld from children and young people; Respect for the individual preferences and peculiarities of the child, both in work and in behaviour; Morality and reasoning to arise from the children's actual experience in a democratic group and never of necessity from the authority or convenience of adults.[9]

The Russells had intended that the school should offer a radically different learning experience for their children. Ati quotes Bertrand Russell as saying, "Education must be subversive if it is to be meaningful. By this I mean that it must challenge all the things we take for granted, examine all accepted assumptions, tamper with every sacred cow, and instill a desire to question and doubt."

Dora Russell said that schools for the privileged in England reinforced "the obtuseness and the brutality of privilege toward those who have it not." In contrast, schools for the working class instructed children "up to the exact point at which their instruction makes them adequate citizens, without awakening their initiative and intelligence sufficiently to produce people who are psychic equals of the upper class and might dispute with them for leadership."

Furthermore, the elite, male-only schools developed from a medieval mindset that emphasized religious and moral training, reading and writing, and ultimately hierarchy. Only outside the school does one find "the workshop, the factory, the prairie; the dream of millions of a world where there are not masters and slaves . . . the world of women's thoughts, purposes, rights, loves."[10]

Dora Russell saw democracy as the basic principle of the Beacon Hill School: It "defines each child as a unique individual who belongs, not to the State, or even to his parents, but first of all to himself."[11] For Ati, that ideology was definitely formative in a manner the mirror opposite of National Socialism. Imagine the impact on a ten-year-old. Ati faced schooling one year that demanded conformity to a rigid social order. The next year her schooling encouraged question and doubt. She had to interpret these experiences and make sense of them for her own life.

LEARNING WITH FAMILY AND FRIENDS

In 1937 the family moved again, this time to New England. Ati entered Concord Academy, which was at that time an all-girls prep school. The school's guiding principles had been established by its first head, Elsie Garland Hobson: "excellence without pretension, service to the wider world, and hard work balanced with wholesome recreation." But when Ati entered as part of a class of 15 in 1938, a new head had just begun, Valeria Addams Knapp. Faculty member Marcelia Wagner said, "Miss Knapp was young, breezy. . . . Almost immediately, the school took on a carefree air."[12]

The school lay at yet another pole of education, more conventional than the one at Beacon Hill, but still far removed from her experiences in Germany. The most important learning there occurred with a teacher, but outside of school. After grade six, she was befriended by Marcelia Wagner and would spend weekend afternoons with her. Ati described her house as her "refuge and joy." "Miss Wagner . . . continued to be a mother-figure to me long after I had passed out of her sixth grade class, for she loved me a little bit the way my mother had."

Miss Wagner took Ati on "wondrous outings in her little two-seater Buick that had no heat. She would bundle us up in a fur blanket and off we would set for an afternoon in the Fine Arts or Science museums of Boston where she would astonish me with her curious comments." Miss Wagner had no explicit teaching aims for these outings, yet she provided a "quintessential education," by sharing what she loved in poetry, art, and mathematics.

Miss Wagner created happy times and offered Ati unconditional positive regard:

> To Miss Wagner everything I drew or wrote was a pleasure, and it was my delight to give her things. At home I had come to hide every picture I made in the cellar, not because I was criticized for them, but I could see their inferiority

through the Gropius's eyes. Nothing I made was beautiful or original or talented like all the objects in the house.

For Ati at this time, learning could not be defined in terms of the curriculum within Concord Academy, nor in terms of her extracurricular time with Miss Wagner or the Gropius, but in a rich ecosystem comprising these and the relation between them.

DEMOCRACY AS A WAY OF LIFE

By age 16, as Ati matured, she also had conflicts with her parents. Not knowing exactly what to do with her, they considered Black Mountain College[13] near Asheville, North Carolina. The college had opened just a few years earlier. Walter Gropius had deep connections through his colleagues at Bauhaus, a German art and design school that combined crafts and fine arts. He and Marcel Breuer designed the studies building there. But the college chose a simpler design by Lawrence Kocher since it was students, working with faculty, who needed to do the actual construction.

The college soon became a famous center for education and the arts, including hosting Buckminster Fuller's first geodesic dome, and early performances by Merce Cunningham and John Cage. Alma Stone became the first African American student to attend an all-white college in the Jim Crow South, ten years before the *Brown v. Board of Education* decision by the Supreme Court.

Black Mountain's founder, John Andrew Rice, conceived the school as a revolt against higher education of its day. It emphasized employing the arts to support learning across the disciplines, social and cultural activities beyond the classroom, experiential learning, and democratic governance. "If there was a single unquestionable assumption underlying the college's structure and philosophy, it was a belief in democracy as a way of life."[14]

Through its ideology and sharing of specific participants, such as Josef (known as Juppi) and Anni Albers, it was in many ways America's Bauhaus.[15] Both used the idea of design as a means for building a better world, but also a means for investigating larger issues of knowledge, community, and democracy.

Ati was hesitant to enroll at first. Seeing photos of students working in the fields, she connected that with her understanding of slavery on Southern plantations or prison camps: "I had arrived at the work camp of my worst fears. Why was it then that 48 hours later I had no intention of ever leaving the place?"

The labor force turned out to be students and faculty who had volunteered for work that needed doing, such as "hoeing corn, shoveling coal, whitewashing walls." Ati soon became a happy participant in the small Black

Mountain community: "You felt immediately that . . . you were not in a category called 'student,' but you were part of a very alive community, where everybody was on the same level."[16] She saw that her work mattered and so did her opinion. Overnight she was transformed from a teenager into an adult.

Black Mountain was an experiment in education, in which *community* played a central role. It strived to be non-hierarchical and accepting of diversity in methods, theories, and personalities. But things were not always smooth. During Ati's second summer there (1944), friction between the "arts and education" and the "scholarship and politics" camps erupted into what was called a "civil war." The impact on Ati was profound: "It was my first exposure to politics, group pressures, opinion manipulation, rhetoric, distortions, power plays, and the polarization had gripped the student body. . . . No cause was ever able to attract me again. On the other hand I had also learned to observe exemplary behavior and ethics in action."

The apparent failure of community was perhaps more significant for her learning than the earlier smoothly functioning community had been. It helped define her ethical stance for a lifetime and taught her to be responsible for her own beliefs. It also attracted her to Charles Forberg, for his "insight" and "detached judgement," which gave him "the stature of an Abraham Lincoln." She married him after the Black Mountain years.

Ati interpreted the Black Mountain "civil war" in a way that shaped her developing self, her identity, and her values, just as it might for any of us. One of her fellow students might have had an equally strong reaction, but a divergent interpretation, leading them to turn away from detachment and self-responsibility toward politics and social change. Another might have been less aware that the power plays and polarization even existed. The incident reveals our very human capacity to make sense of experience and thereby shape the possibilities for our own futures.

The term *community* at Black Mountain was used to refer to the 100 or so residents. But John Wallen, a twenty-seven-year-old faculty member, insisted that Black Mountain's isolation from its local setting was a scandal: It operated as if it were not in a specific time and space.[17] For Wallen, *community* should include both what went on inside and relations with the outside neighbors.

Ati responded positively to both the freedom that Black Mountain encouraged and the responsibility that it demanded. Schools such as Black Mountain seek to accept the diversity of learners, not only across broad categories such as race or class, but also in terms of individual learning styles and interests. They also place greater responsibility in the hands of learners.

This means that the actual outcome of education is not easily predicted and may diverge from a core curriculum defined by specific knowledge and skills. For Ati, legitimate participation in community enabled her to move from the freedom to learn to becoming a responsible leader.

Ati describes many teachers who influenced her at Black Mountain, not only in traditional academic areas, but in moral development and character formation. The idea of making things was pervasive, whether in the fields or in art class. There was also a belief in the value of careful observation, which Ati incorporated into her own mode of being in the world: "The focus was entirely on learning the marvels of the world around us and we were asked simply to give full attention." She cites Josef Albers, whose aim was to open eyes, as her strongest influence.

CONNECTING LEARNING TO LIFE

In addition to her formal schooling, Ati had other models to inform her worldview. Her uncle and aunt, Walter Gropius and Ise Gropius, had founded the Bauhaus school of design and movement, which is generally viewed as one of Weimar's major cultural achievements.[18] Although Ati said later that she did not have any idea of the Bauhaus philosophy, it surely influenced her thinking, especially after her mother died, when Ati was nine. She was then adopted by her mother's sister, Ise Frank, and her uncle, Walter Gropius, from whom she learned even more of the Bauhaus approach.

During its fifteen years, Bauhaus had three locations—Weimar, Dessau, and Berlin—and three different architect-directors. Not surprisingly, its mission, focus, and practices shifted several times and there were competing theories, visions, and designs. But there were some common themes throughout. Walter Gropius said that "the aim of the Bauhaus was not a style, or a system, or a canon or prescription or fashion. It will be alive as long as it does not cling to form but seeks the fluidity of life beyond all mutable forms."[19]

In a study of the Bauhaus educational philosophy, Anita Cross writes that Gropius envisaged "a craft-orientated, unified scheme of instruction which incorporated some of the social principles of the Dewey scheme, the Froebelian respect for individual freedom and controlled creativity, and the craft emphasis of the English Arts reform movement proposed by Ruskin and Morris."[20]

The Bauhaus philosophy entailed a focus on materials, rather than adherence to a predetermined style, with an emphasis on local resources, including the steel and glass of the industrial age; interdisciplinary learning; experimentation; the fusion of arts with crafts; function over form; avoidance of unnecessary ornamentation; a deep understanding of color and design; and other features viewed by most people today as defining modernism.

Many items in common use today exemplify Bauhaus: lever door handles, chairs with an S-shaped tubular steel design, abstract painting for utility textiles, Anglepoise lamps, chess sets, and functional, total design reflecting modern industry. Bauhaus wallpaper is still popular and once funded the entire school.

Despite these designs epitomizing modernism, Bauhaus insiders, including Ati, would say that interpreting Bauhaus as the modern style reveals a misunderstanding of its central tenets. If anything, it was anti-style, and instead an approach to both education and design that valued experimentation and clear attention to materials, function, and design principles.

Ati wrote that Ise was Walter's "Venus without whom his heart would have had no center. Sometimes viewed as a hard edged geometrist of white boxes, the godfather of the white cube, he was actually a true romantic by nature. This expressed itself in all his personal lives and in his deep bonding with nature, music, poetry, and all the arts."[21]

Bauhaus opposed the very idea of style for its own sake, emphasizing instead situated, functional responses to immediate problems. Upon arriving at Harvard in 1937, Walter Gropius was explicit about his intention:

> [It] is not to introduce a . . . "Modern Style" from Europe, but rather to introduce a method of approach which allows one to tackle a problem according to its peculiar conditions . . . to make young people realize how inexhaustible the means of creation are if they make use of the innumerable products of our age, and to encourage these young people in finding their own solutions.[22]

Ignoring Gropius's intention, many people, who might be stumped when asked to distinguish Queen Anne style from Queen Victorian, or Baroque from rococo, would feel that the one style they could pick out is the modern style, and some would go further to identify it as the Bauhaus style (or the international style, the functional style). They might even identify Gropius as the inventor of this very definite style.

During one meeting, historian Mark Steinberg and Ati argued over this concept of style. Mark insisted that style meant essentially a set of practices, a cultural formation. Modernism in the arts was a definite movement, with a recognizable style, which emerged partly in reaction to World War I and more generally to the development of modern industrial societies and urbanization. Ati stressed that the Bauhaus movement *was* central to modernism, but that people missed its vital contributions—its valorization of learning, experimentation, community, and democracy when they viewed it as a style. She had incorporated those Bauhaus values into her own approach to learning and life and, in turn, brought them into her teaching (and arguments in the living room).

This was a potential learning opportunity, one that Bauhaus might have missed. In what ways might a concerted effort against style itself become a style? What does style really mean? Could a focus on design not only seek to improve design per se, but help people engage with larger questions of aesthetics or social philosophy?

Gropius also insisted upon the larger education mission of the Bauhaus and of designers, architects, and artists in general. It was crucial to nurture "the individual's capacity to seek and understand the deeper potentialities of life."[23] These ideas were salient in the Gropius family and contributed to Ati's understanding of learning.

Bauhaus was many things. But throughout there was experimentation, a focus on lived experience, and a belief in each person's creative potential. In contrast to the rigid and isolated schooling of its time, Bauhaus offered a vibrant, richly nourished, and ecosystems-aware approach to learning. This approach was evident in Ati's own approach to learning and life.

LEARNING AND TEACHING

Ati grew to become an illustrator of children's books, a graphic designer, and a teacher, roles that each reflected her diverse educational background. She was known for her independent thinking and passion for learning and teaching. These attitudes persisted until her death at age 88 in 2014.

Ati was a lifelong teacher as well as being a learner. At various colleges, museums,[24] and libraries, she taught her version of the Bauhaus Lab, a miniature of the Bauhaus first-year foundation course, as taught by Josef Albers. Ati might start by placing one sheet of blank paper in the center of a table and tell participants to talk about it. Like Albers, she would open up their perception with "What do you see?" Students might note that the paper is flat, thin, white, has four sides, or has 90-degree angles. She would ask, "How is it lying? If this were a person, what would you find yourself doing to it?"

After further discussion, she would ask students to create the biggest change in the paper with the least action. One might fold it neatly in half; another might fold on a diagonal; another might roll it, or tear it. As they shared their changes, Ati would engage the students, encouraging them to use their hands and expand on their creations. The paper might become a tent, a sail, a seagull, or a building. With more slits and folds the variety and the insights would continue to expand. This is the beginning of a process that Ati and, earlier, Bauhaus used to engage students with the principles of design.

LIFELONG LEARNING

One day, when she was well into her 80s, Ati called on the phone. The conversation proceeded as follows:

Ati: I'd like to talk with you about philosophy of education.

The author: OK, where shall we meet? Your house? Mine? The library?

Ati: Let's go to the beach.

The beach prevailed. Ati took off her shoes so she could walk barefoot in the sand. A three-mile walk had room for Bauhaus, Josef Albers, Bertrand Russell, Dewey, and the relation of arts to education. This kind of event was typical for her.

Not long afterward, she instigated the formation of a weekly philosophy seminar. This was held in members' homes, which began with the question: What is consciousness? Following a meandering path, over several months, participants read the Cambridge Declaration on Consciousness, which states that a significant number of non-human animals are conscious beings. They also read works of Philippe Descola, René Girard, Alan Watts, and William James. They discussed the meaning of beauty, Chinese philosophy, the interpretation of poetry, scapegoats, and brain science.

Although privileged in many ways, Ati also faced upheavals and struggles throughout her life, which challenged her identity and values. One result was that she became self-reliant and independent in her thinking. She held strong opinions and could back them up with rich life experiences. She was unafraid to challenge orthodoxies, relying instead on her own experiences and reasoning.

SUMMARY

In Ati's biography, formal learning is linked in multiple ways with other problems and activities, such as those that arise in parental work, libraries, and the economic, social, cultural, and political currents of the larger society. Her learning is a product of the education ecosystem, within which she co-creates learning niches. Unplanned experience, such as the "civil war" at Black Mountain College, had profound effects on her learning, beyond many of the intentional learning experiences.

When asked about which type of education she preferred, she expressed clear preferences. Yet she also said that she learned things from every situation. In some cases, such as her earliest formal schooling in Berlin, she may have learned more than she realized or cared to.

Throughout these diverse experiences, Ati was not simply a vessel to be filled with knowledge. The way that she interpreted her experiences shaped to a large extent what they meant to her and for her learning. Her work with Josef Albers is notable in this regard. His credo of opening eyes became central to her own teaching and to her learning, long after Black Mountain College. He undoubtedly said and taught many things, but for her the request to give full attention to "the marvels of the world around us" was most salient. As one example, it surely connected with her lifelong interest in stars, galaxies, solstices, and equinoxes.

Ati's educational biography also shows the importance of engaged, meaningful participation in some rich activity, such as visiting a museum or carrying out an arts project. That provides the soil in which specific learning can grow. Although Ati claimed that it was possible to learn in any situation, one can see in her comments and writing how much that potential could be enhanced when she had the desire to participate and when she could connect that situation with other experiences with parents, friends, mentors, and creative life.

NOTES

1. Plutarch, *Essays*, trans. Robin Waterfield (New York: Penguin Classics, 1992), 50.

2. Jean Umiker-Sebeok, "Meaning Construction in a Cultural Gallery: A Sociosemiotic Study of Consumption Experiences in a Museum," in *Advances in Consumer Research*, vol. 19, ed. John F. Sherry Jr. and Brian Sternthal (Provo, UT: Association for Consumer Research, 1992), 46–55.

3. Clifford Geertz, *The Interpretation of Cultures: Selected Essays* (New York: Basic Books, 1973), 5, building on the ideas of the influential early sociologist Max Weber.

4. Henry Adams, *The Education of Henry Adams* (Boston: Houghton Mifflin, [1907] 1948), 379.

5. Yrjö Engeström, *Learning by Expanding: An Activity-Theoretical Approach to Developmental Research*, 2nd ed. (Cambridge: Cambridge University Press, 2014).

6. Ati lived near the author in a Bauhaus-inspired house with her architect husband, John Johansen. There were many discussions in which she reflected on education in general and on her own learning process.

7. A detailed account of Ati's world is conveyed in Fiona MacCarthy's *Gropius: The Man Who Built the Bauhaus* (Cambridge, MA: Harvard University Press, 2019).

8. Ati Gropius Johansen, "An English Education," Dora Winifred Russell Papers (Amsterdam, The Netherlands: International Institute of Social History, 1985). See also *Interview with Ati Johansson Gropius*, by Sigrid Pawelke, video, 2010, Black Mountain Research. Unless indicated otherwise, the discussion and quotations in this chapter are from unpublished writings generously made available by her family or from conversations with Ati and her daughter Erika Pfammatter.

9. Quoted by Deborah Gorham in "Dora and Bertrand Russell and Beacon Hill School," *Journal of Bertrand Russell Studies* 25, no. 1 (Summer 2005): 47.

10. All Dora Russell quotes from *In Defence of Children* (London, UK: Hamish Hamilton, 1932), 236–37.

11. Ibid., 42.

12. Concord Academy, "Past Heads," accessed August 30, 2019, https://concordacademy.org/about/history/past-heads.

13. Katherine Chaddock Reynolds, *Visions and Vanities: John Andrew Rice of Black Mountain College* (Baton Rouge: Louisiana State University Press, 1998).

14. Mary Emma Harris, *The Arts at Black Mountain College* (Cambridge, MA: MIT Press, 2002), 7.

15. JoAnn C. Ellert, "The Bauhaus and Black Mountain College," *The Journal of General Education* 24, no. 3 (October 1972): 144–52; Karl Heinz Füssl, "Pestalozzi in Dewey's Realm? Bauhaus Master Josef Albers among the German-Speaking Emigrés' Colony at Black Mountain College (1933–1949)," *Paedagogica Historica* 42, no. 1–2 (2006): 77–92.

16. Sigrid Pawelke, *Interview with Ati Johansson Gropius* (2010).

17. Martin Duberman, *Black Mountain: An Exploration in Community* (Evanston, IL: Northwestern University Press, 2009), 250.

18. Bauhaus celebrated its centennial in 2019.

19. Ati Gropius Johansen, *Walter Gropius: The Man Behind the Ideas* (Boston: Historic New England, 2012), 24.

20. Anita Cross, "The Educational Background to the Bauhaus," *Design Studies* 4, no. 1 (1983): 48. Friedrich Froebel had founded an institute for early childhood education in Germany. He designed Froebel Gifts, or *Fröbelgaben*, which included geometric building blocks and pattern activity blocks. His building forms and movement games inspired Bauhaus, and Gropius later designed the Friedrich Fröbel Haus in Berlin. William Morris was a leading proponent of the Arts and Crafts movement, which stressed traditional craftsmanship using simple forms. That movement meshed well with John Ruskin's social critique, and both were significant influences on Bauhaus, especially on eliding the distinction between fine arts and useful crafts and deprecating ornamentation.

21. Johansen, *Walter Gropius: The Man Behind the Ideas*, 1.

22. Walter Gropius, *Scope of Total Architecture* (New York: Collier, 1943), 17.

23. Ibid., 13.

24. Alexandra Lange, "Hands-On: The Gropius Touch," *New York Times*, January 20, 2010.

Chapter Nine

A Dialogue on Formal and Informal Learning

> The acquisition of knowledge always involves the revelation of ignorance. . . . All our problems tend to gather under two questions about knowledge: Having the ability and desire to know, how and what should we learn? And, having learned, how and for what should we use what we know?
>
> —Wendell Berry [1]

Education is rife with great debates over issues such as its overall purpose, how to teach reading, whether to emphasize jobs or general education, how to foster moral developments, what technologies to use, incorporation of the arts, and much more. This is an unavoidable and never-ending consequence of its centrality to life and the values we hold. Education's ecosystem is also the ecosystem of human life.

One such debate is that between education as a formal procedure and what is usually called informal education. The former is instantiated in classrooms, textbooks, learning objectives, formal assessment, lectures, and other apparatus of formal education. The latter is seen as the by-product of activity. It may include accidental forms of learning, but more commonly purposeful learning in contexts other than classrooms, such as a summer camp or on-the-job training.

Some would emphasize the formal side as necessary for developing a shared culture or for building capacity to cope with complex problems in the modern era. Others would emphasize the informal, seeing it as more "natural," and supporting more direct links between theory and practice.

The advent of new media and online learning, alternative modes of certification, and the need for lifelong learning make it increasingly difficult to say exactly what school-based versus informal, or experiential, learning is today. Moreover, formal education usually includes some informal aspects, while experiential or informal education can be highly structured, sometimes with memorization and ritual more formal than any classroom.

However one leans in this debate, even to some kind of hybrid position, views about what the term *education* includes shape our answers to fundamental questions about learning. If we frame learning as school based, then we start with the school (or college, university, summer institute, corporate training center, etc.). This typically leads to an *atomized model* in which we identify the basic units of curricular knowledge or skills. These are the underlying components, like subatomic particles in the physical world. We then seek efficient ways to instill those.

In contrast, some argue for experiential learning and have little interest in the formal structures of learning, which they see as obsolete, or even damaging. Their mantra is for incidental learning as it occurs through daily life experiences, work, and play. This is usually, though not always, a more holistic and open approach to learning. Accordingly, it invites the criticism that it neglects systematic instruction on the building blocks of knowledge.

Let us explore the consequences of the two models through a dialogue between two figures from ancient mythology, Athena and Artemis: With her bust gracing many school lobbies, *Athena*, the Greek goddess of wisdom, represents here the atomized learning model. Clearly, wisdom if it comes at all, arises in many different ways, but we will focus on Athena's role as a guide for formal education. *Artemis*, the goddess of the hunt, wild animals, and wilderness, represents the experiential learning model.

The dialogue is organized around a dozen questions:

1. *Who* learns (and who teaches)?
2. *What* is learned?
3. *Where* does learning occur?
4. *When* does learning occur?
5. *Why* do people learn?
6. *How* do people learn?
7. How does education *prepare us* for life?
8. How do we *measure success*?
9. How should schools *relate to the outside world*?
10. What is the role of *literacy*?
11. How can we learn *abstract ideas*?
12. Should the *community be the curriculum*?

WHO LEARNS (AND WHO TEACHES)?

Athena: The answer to the *who* question is that education is primarily about students in a school, usually young ones, who study a prescribed curriculum under the direction of a teacher. In this model, students begin as empty vessels and gradually accumulate important knowledge. This follows from a technical definition of education as an intentional process whereby a society transmits values, knowledge, and skills to the next generation.

Artemis: There are many problems with that formal transmission model: First of all, society cannot transmit values, knowledge, and skills by simply telling them. Its efforts to do so are often ineffective or even counterproductive, as learners interpret and reconstruct ideas in light of their own experiences. Everyone is a potential learner all the time.

WHAT IS LEARNED?

Athena: Because education is school based, its content needs to be packaged into textbooks, curricula, and corresponding assessment tools. This most often means clearly defined units of knowledge and testable skills.

The precise format of lessons varies, but generally students learn best through well-planned lessons. The lesson planner must first clearly state objectives, or learning goals, then specify necessary materials in advance, then lay out a step-by-step procedure, which all students can follow, and define an assessment procedure to ensure that the objectives have been met. The procedure typically includes clear explanations of basic terms and questions, modeling, and activities that incrementally build toward mastery of basic concepts.

Standards are set by schools, districts, states, and nations to provide an overarching framework for individual lessons. For example in the United States, the Common Core Standards are an effort to set high-quality academic standards in mathematics and English language arts/literacy for students regardless of which state they live in. The learning goals outline what a student should know and be able to do at the end of each grade.[2]

Artemis: Athena's approach defines learning goals a priori, often in terms of abstractions. Freire calls this the *banking model*, in which "knowledge is a gift bestowed by those who consider themselves knowledgeable upon those whom they consider to know nothing."[3]

The teacher talks about reality as if it were motionless, static, compartmentalized, and predictable. Or else he expounds on a topic completely alien to the existential experience of the students. His task is to "fill" the students with the contents of his narration-contents, which are detached from reality, disconnected from the totality that engendered them and could give them significance. Words are emptied of their concreteness and become a hollow, alienated, and alienating verbosity.[4]

In the banking model, the learning process is structured hierarchically, flowing from the teacher to the student, and from the curriculum to the student's acquisition of decontextualized knowledge. The textbook and the lecture play a central role.

Few people successfully fill much of their brain with facts from sitting in a classroom. All too often, classroom activities are purely receptive and call for limited engagement, they are divorced from the storehouse of experiences students bring from everyday life, they lack significance in the students' world, and the context of learning is too far removed from potential contexts of application.

WHERE DOES LEARNING OCCUR?

Athena: Education is the formal style of learning and encompasses its major aspects. Outside-of-school learning occurs, of course, but our institution of schooling provides not only procedures to support learning, but common standards, sequencing, and criteria for success.

Artemis: Even in the school, the most significant learning may happen in hallways, playgrounds, or enrichment activities, such as project work.

Education systems around the world often teach mostly decontextualized skills and knowledge, separated from work, play, and community life. The process is shaped by a testing industry focusing on narrowly defined measurements that fail to reflect what learning does occur. If one begins to think instead in terms of human growth and flourishing, or of the linkages between schooling and other aspects of life, or of the relation between learning and democratic living, then that system deserves failing grades.

We should consider *de-schooling*, as Ivan Illich writes. He argues that the oppressive structure of the school system cannot be reformed. It is both a consequence of and a contributor to the lifelong institutionalization in society.[5] The disestablishment of schools is not a proposal for privatization, as some contemporary critics espouse; it is instead a fundamental rejection of schooling within institutionalized culture.[6]

WHEN DOES LEARNING OCCUR?

Athena: Learning occurs within a precisely defined time frame. Often (in the United States), school starts in September and ends in May, except for special sessions during the summer. Each week, usually Monday through Friday, has a rhythm. For example, enrichment activities tend to occur on Friday afternoon, if at all. Each day has a schedule with uniform start and end times.

The higher one goes in grade levels, the more subject areas are differentiated. There is little overlap; history is not allowed to intrude in science class, or vice versa. Even in primary school, subject areas should be marked off. Math often happens in the morning, when the pupils are most awake. Science and social studies happen in the afternoon.

Artemis: The time frame for learning is important, but only in limited situations, such as a school or in a seminar. More often, learning is space framed, if it is framed at all; we learn in different settings, not different hours. There is not so much need to separate subject areas.

WHY DO PEOPLE LEARN?

Athena: The goal of education is to prepare students for careers, or as an intermediate step for the next level of schooling. For example, primary school readies students for middle school, which in turn readies them for high school. High school readies them for college or for a career that does not require a college degree.

Artemis: Formal education operates in an as-if world. When students are asked to write a persuasive essay, they write as if they were trying to persuade someone. When they calculate distance from rate and time, they do so as if it mattered how far they would go at a particular rate for a given time. When they vote for class president, they manufacture issues as if their social relations depended in a crucial way upon the class governance.

Education has become a self-referential system. People now talk about academic readiness for kindergarten, or even preschool. It is time to step back to ask what is the purpose of the entire enterprise. The goal appears to be stacking up bricks made of knowledge bits or isolated skills. Instead, we learn from daily life, in order to enhance our capacity for further life and learning.

HOW DO PEOPLE LEARN?

Athena: Students learn from good teaching, based on time-tested schemas. Jack Easley articulates several of these in an article on teachers' schemas for teaching: Teachers should regularly lead class discussions, present clear explanations and examples of basic concepts, and/or ask questions so that students can piece together the principles desired. They should master their subjects prior to trying to teach them. They can and should transmit their knowledge to students. They should present simple and easy problems and tasks in order to build pupils' courage to tackle more difficult and unfamiliar tasks.[7]

Regardless of the teaching assumptions, learning is serious business, clearly to be distinguished from fun, which happens at recess, or before and after school. The focus is on cognitive skills and testable knowledge. Aesthetics is a means to improve knowledge transfer. Even when considering literature, the aim is to "get the main idea" or understand "sequencing," not to expand on one's own personal response or to make judgments that might lead to, say, rejection of the required text.

Artemis: As reasonable as the Easley schemas may appear at first reading, his article proceeds to debunk all of them, and four similar schemas as well. Easley sees learning as a process of constructing knowledge. This leads him to question each of the assumptions.

For example, clear explanations may seem to be desirable, but what is clear to the teacher may be opaque to a learner new to the subject area. Moreover, hearing a summative statement about some phenomena may discourage any effort to puzzle it out on one's own. The resulting knowledge is hollow or fragile since it is not based on the experience of problem solving in life.

Furthermore, Easley questions the presumption of the teacher as the leader of discussions, finding instead that small-group discussions can be productive in many cases. Also, as valuable as talk may be, it should be coupled with hands-on investigations wherever possible. Easley continues in this vein for each of eight assumptions, showing how studies of actual learning lead to reconsideration of many "obvious" principles for teaching.

HOW DOES EDUCATION PREPARE US FOR LIFE?

Athena: Although the ultimate purpose is to prepare students for careers, civic responsibilities, and self-development, schooling can address those aims only indirectly. We need instead to emphasize specific knowledge and skills that can be presented in curricular materials, taught efficiently, and assessed fairly and accurately. We start students early in life because there is so much to learn.

Artemis: The best preparation is lifelong learning. This means being fully engaged in the present moment, not attempting to accumulate knowledge with little meaning and relevance. The complexity of life and never-ending change means that education cannot be reduced to a formulaic preparation for living. Charles Sanders Peirce recognized this in his articulation of pragmatist theory, which was a major influence on William James and others, whose work in turn influenced progressive educators.

Education must allow for messiness and creativity, emphasizing not instruction in specific knowledge and skills, but instead an environment that enhances the capacity to live fully and to make sense of experience. We should "cease conceiving of education as mere preparation for later life, and make it the full meaning of the present life."[8]

HOW DO WE MEASURE SUCCESS?

Athena: Success is measured at the student level primarily by standardized tests, which assess the understanding of key concepts. There are similar content exams in places where standardized testing has not been implemented yet. The concepts to be tested are identified through a complex system of curricular development and review, test item construction, and correlations across schools, districts, states, and nations. It is crucial to make the process quantifiable, and consistent across years and settings. Among other things, this produces a level playing field for learners; teachers, parents, and students know how success will be measured.

For teachers, schools, districts, states, and nations, the individual student results percolate up. We can then make comparisons, such as that Japan does better in math, but New Zealand does better in literacy. The results are high stakes because student progress, teacher jobs, school funding, real estate prices, placement of new industries all depend on them.

Criteria for evaluating schools typically include

- modern facilities, commodious for learning, even beautiful;
- use of the latest and best new technologies;
- production of workers ideally suited for the future employment;
- like-minded parents, and children with similar interests, backgrounds, and abilities;
- high performance on standardized tests, regardless of starting point; and
- excellence for those of special merit.

Artemis: Alfred North Whitehead stated the problem well, nearly a century ago:

> Every school is bound on pain of extinction to train its [students] for a small set of definite examinations. No headmaster has a free hand to develop his general education or his specialist studies in accordance with the opportunities of his school. . . . No system of external tests which aims primarily at examining individual scholars can result in anything but educational waste.[9]

Across various cultures and time periods, people have held purposes for education beyond performance on atomized exams. These include developing individuals who can participate fully in diverse life activities including family life, become socially engaged citizens, satisfy their intellectual curiosity, love learning, appreciate arts and music, learn right from wrong, and learn how to get along with others.[10]

Athena's view of educational quality focuses on inputs, such as the latest technology, physical facilities, and up-to-date curricula, or on outputs, most typically job placement or scores on standardized tests. The implicit emphasis on individual achievement reflects the narrow conception of evolution as survival of the fittest. And that is what it becomes for individual students, teachers, families, and others caught in a dehumanizing system. The system is designed to produce failures. Privileging competition to the exclusion of communication, cooperation, and construction hinders achievement of the social goals of education as well as harms individuals.

HOW SHOULD SCHOOLS RELATE TO THE OUTSIDE WORLD?

Athena: Modern schooling seeks to ensure that knowledge, reasoning, and problem solving are based on abstract, generalizable, even universal understanding. Knowledge creation and utilization is henceforth removed from the messiness of ordinary life. Their power derives precisely from that liberation. By standing apart from everyday life, education can serve to analyze it, reflect upon it, enhance it, or correct it.

Life in the outside world is, of course, essential to consider for schooling. What students bring to school shapes their experience, probably more than anything the teacher can do. And the aim is to prepare the student for that outside world. Schools should thus learn to take advantage of field trips, local parks, nature centers, libraries, and other resources, but ultimately the responsibility for learning rests on the school. It is difficult to show that the effort to do these extracurricular activities pays off in terms of school success, which is defined by test scores.

Artemis: Schooling and life can never be fully separated, even if we try to do so. Both the problems and the resources of the larger society shape the kinds of schools we create. This occurs both from society to school, and from school to society. We support universal schooling because we know that education impacts every aspect of life, universal citizenship, and every vocation. For this reason, it can be the scapegoat, as suggested above, or the panacea for societal ills.

The converse is true as well: Each problem in society implies a problem for education. For example, if racism is structural in society, it necessarily leads to racism in the organization, funding, and operation of schools. Similarly, the resources of the larger society provide the resources for learning.

WHAT IS THE ROLE OF LITERACY?

Athena: Reading is essential to learning. We learn to read, then read to learn. In the modern era we may need to expand the definition of reading to include reading hypertexts, videos, diagrams, data sets, and more, but the core idea of absorbing far more than we could ever experience directly remains.

Academic study provides language for describing experiences, thereby improving our capacity to reflect more deeply upon them. Think of Galileo observing small white spots through his telescope, then going on to conceive of moons circling the planet Jupiter. The discipline of astronomy, even in its early days, offered ways to characterize images, spheres, orbits, temporal patterns, and more, enabling Galileo to articulate his findings and future generations to discuss and comprehend them.

Academic study also empowers us to think in terms of past and future, and to connect with the experiences of others. Our own inquiry can thereby be linked with and compared to the inquiry of others, both contemporaneously and through the accumulated understandings represented in disciplinary knowledge. Formal study also offers a space to consider hypothetical situations that extend and test our understanding.

Artemis: The very power of reading can lead us to replace dialogue, interaction with the physical and biological world, visual art, music, dance, community engagement, and the many other ways that people learn. However, literacy itself derives from that complex ecosystem. For example, children use letters, texts, and other communication as a means of learning sociability and building relationships, learning to read and write while employing literacy to reinforce those social relations.[11] The new literacies movements could be described as an effort to understand how literacy is not an alternative to, but a vital part of, general life experience.[12]

HOW CAN WE LEARN ABSTRACT IDEAS?

Athena: Direct experience is fine for some kinds of learning, but it does not help for learning about, say, calculus or the lives of the ancient Egyptians. We ought to be restoring a knowledge-based curriculum so that we can enable everyone to possess a common culture, most of which cannot be experienced directly.[13]

Formal education does operate in an as-if world. There are actually many good reasons to do so. We can only occasionally learn through direct interaction with the world. Until we develop interplanetary travel it will not be possible to study all aspects of potential life on Mars through direct experience. We cannot even experience other cultures on Earth. Whether to consider the view through a telescope as direct is a matter of debate. And until we have time travel, our experience of, say, the Roaring Twenties, will be severely limited, at best simulated. Even when we might in principle engage students in direct experience of some phenomena, such as operating a nuclear power plant, it seems wise not to do so.

As a result, we know that education necessarily involves reports from others, usually represented in books, charts, websites, videos, simulations, and such. Models, idealizations, and approximations are an integral part of everyday procedure in science (taken broadly). We need to create useful fictions, for example, by any pictorial presentation of data. Collective thought progresses through the creation of these fictions.

Artemis: When we base learning on lived experiences in the community around us, we do not exclude arcane problems in higher mathematics, details of linguistics, or obscure corners of history. Instead, we embed them in situations with relevance and complexity that make the learning more meaningful.

In Dora Whitaker's primary grade classroom, children began by measuring their own bodies. They graphed changes and comparisons to adult dimensions as a starting point for discussing growth.[14] They also listened to portions of *Gulliver's Travels* and asked whether Jonathan Swift computed the size of Gulliver's suit accurately.

Through activities such as these they expanded the possibilities for learning. Mathematics came alive as they saw how it is a language for discussing growth, plants, literature, patterns, and everyday life. Whitaker showed that young children can engage even with calculus early in their school career, once they are allowed to build upon concrete activities.

SHOULD THE COMMUNITY BE THE CURRICULUM?

Athena: Learning cannot be reduced to contemporary community activities. It should encompass far-off communities and ideas from long ago, not only what is happening in the local neighborhood. A focus on community can lead to conformity, rigidity, and xenophobia. When we make the community become the curriculum we can reinforce divisions, reifying segregation and hierarchy. Privatization of schools, charters, gated communities, and home schooling have exacerbated this tendency.

These consequences of community are very real pathologies. But some of the most pernicious effects of community come from what we imagine. Benedict Anderson details how *imagined communities* lay the basis for nationalism, and ultimately war. It is easy to see how imagined communities within a large high school can be supportive to some and injurious to others. The community we imagine, an extended comradeship, potentially reinforces ethnic prejudice, nationalism, and even the willingness to kill or die.[15]

Artemis: When the community is the curriculum, learning becomes relevant and applicable to life. In addition, many have understood how important it can be to reach out to the neighborhood communities of students, finding both unrecognized resources and problems for inquiry.[16] Thus, the culture of learning extends beyond the classroom walls. It is especially crucial to recognize community *funds of knowledge* for those whose cultural resources have been marginalized by traditional curricula.[17]

Education needs to be connected to life because it is the means by which we reflect upon, reproduce, or transform our modes of living. Freire's focus on problem-posing education in contrast to the banking model is a clear antecedent.[18] Earlier, Freinet provided a clear representation of community as curriculum through his learning walks in which students became journalists.[19]

SUMMARY

A thorough examination of the diversity of learning shows that we need to have both rich and varied experience through daily living and the opportunities for reflection which formal learning can provide. There is value in delving into the concrete and particular, to connecting to holistic, primary experiences. That aspect of learning is increasingly lost to our mutual detriment. But there is also value in stepping back, analyzing, abstracting, and simplifying to deduce general principles.

We need ways to connect experience and reflection. The interactions between informal and formal learning often matter more than the specific learning within one arena. When a student enters a classroom, they may be expected to assume a new role, but they cannot shed their prior experiences, beliefs, values, hopes, or fears. Conversely, students take their in-school experiences with them into their outside-of-school lives.

Most discussions of education gloss over the integration of reflection with everyday life experience. Some speak as if experience alone, say, hands-on learning, learning by doing, or community participation, is sufficient. Others emphasize only the reflection on meaning, implicitly defining real learning as separating oneself from ordinary experiences. The discussion then reduces to formal classroom procedures removed from ordinary life versus practical experience devoid of reflection and connection to the larger record of inquiry. Occasionally, reflection is introduced as a stand-alone routine. In each case, the link between experience and reflection is lost. When that link is severed, education becomes hollow, meaningless, and useless for either acting in the world or making sense of it.

NOTES

1. Wendell Berry, *The Art of the Commonplace: The Agrarian Essays of Wendell Berry* (Berkeley, CA: Counterpoint, 2003), 183.
2. Common Core State Standards Initiative, "Preparing America's Students for Success," 2018, http://www.corestandards.org/.
3. Paulo Freire, *Pedagogy of the Oppressed* (New York: Continuum, 1970), 72.
4. Ibid., 57.
5. Ivan Illich, *Deschooling Society* (New York: Harper & Row, 1971).
6. Ivan Illich, *After Deschooling, What?* (London: Writers and Readers Publishing Cooperative, 1976), 48.
7. "A Teacher Educator's Perspective on Students' and Teachers' Schemes," in *Thinking: The Second International Conference*, ed. D. N. Perkins, Jack Lochhead, and John Bishop (Hillsdale, NJ: Lawrence Erlbaum Associates, 2015), 1–19. It must be noted that Easley uses the statement of the schemes as a foil for critiquing them.
8. John Dewey, "Self-Realization as the Moral Ideal," 1893, EW 4:50.
9. Alfred North Whitehead, *The Aims of Education and Other Essays* (New York: Macmillan, 1929), 25.
10. Woon Park, "Modernity and Views of Education: A Comparative Study of Three Countries," *Comparative Education Review* 24, no. 1 (February 1980), 35.
11. Emily Claire Bruce, "Reading Agency: The Making of Modern German Childhoods in the Age of Revolutions," PhD diss., University of Minnesota, 2015.
12. Julie Coiro et al., *Handbook of Research on New Literacies* (New York: Routledge, 2014).
13. E. D. Hirsch, *Why Knowledge Matters: Rescuing Our Children from Failed Educational Theories* (Cambridge, MA: Harvard Education Press, 2016).
14. Dora Whitaker, *Will Gulliver's suit fit? Mathematical Problem-Solving with Children* (Cambridge: Cambridge University Press, 1986).
15. Benedict Anderson, *Imagined Communities: Reflections on the Origin and Spread of Nationalism*, rev. ed. (London: Verso, 1991/2006), 7.
16. Chris Benson and Scott Christian, eds., in *Writing to Make a Difference: Classroom Projects for Community Change* (New York: Teachers College Press, 2002) show how writing projects for students can become more meaningful when connected to community change. Shawn Ginwright, Pablo Noguera, and Julio Cammorota, eds., in *Beyond Resistance! Youth Activism and Community Change* (New York: Routledge, 2006) include reports on how youth can transform their own communities.
17. Luis C. Moll et al., "Funds of Knowledge for Teaching: Using a Qualitative Approach to Connect Homes and Classrooms," *Theory into Practice* 31, no. 2 (October 1, 1992): 132–41.
18. Paulo Freire, *Pedagogy of the Oppressed*, rev. ed., trans. Myra Bergman Ramos (New York: Continuum, [1970] 2005).
19. Victor Acker provides a good biography and summary of Freinet's work in *Célestin Freinet* (Westport, CT: Greenwood, 2000); John Sivell discusses its implementation in Canada in *Freinet Pedagogy: Theory and Practice* (Lewiston, NY and Queenston, Canada: E. Mellen, 1994).

Chapter Ten

The Ecosystem Curriculum

> By ecology, we mean the whole science of the relations of the organism to the environment including, in the broad sense, all the "conditions of existence."... [These include] the physical and chemical properties of its habitat, the climate . . . , inorganic nutrients, nature of the water and of the soil, etc. . . . , [and] the entire relations of the organism to all other organisms with which comes into contact, and which most contribute either to expanded advantage or its harm.
>
> —Ernst Haeckel[1]

The idea that education, or more broadly, learning by any means, occurs in an *ecosystem*, or needs to be examined from an ecological viewpoint is becoming more widely accepted.[2] It has emerged from studies of different contexts for learning, such as classroom versus online, or from comparing on-the-job learning to formal training, as well as from looking at how home and other out-of-classroom experiences shape what occurs in schools.

This book has argued for applying the prism of ecosystems to look at any learning situation. That prism is an analytical tool. It assumes that all learning, just as all life on Earth, exists within some sort of ecosystem. Analyzing how that ecosystem operates can inform us about its effect on an organism. In the case of learning, this analysis can show us much more than we would see from a study of that learning in isolation.

An important question remains: Are some ecosystems better than others? Or more programmatically: Can we specify how to improve education's ecosystem?

Chapter 10
REJECTING THE DICHOTOMIES

The debate between Athena and Artemis in the previous chapter recalls mythological paintings such as Titian's *The Death of Actaeon*, in which Artemis (Diana) transforms Actaeon into a stag and he is mauled by hounds, or David's *The Combat of Ares and Athena*, in which Athena bests Ares in battle and forces him to withdraw to Mount Olympus. Each combatant makes useful points, but ultimately it emerges that there cannot be a victor as in the Greek myths.

Education is at once simpler and far more complex than this debate implies. It is simpler in the sense that underlying all of the diverse theories of perception, memory, and reasoning; the technologies of instruction, assessment, and curriculum design; complex histories and cultural diversity; and the conflicting and ambiguous terminology, there are basic principles about people seeking to survive, and, hopefully, thrive, as they experience life. At the same time, it is more complex because life itself presents us with complexity and unpredictability that belie our most intricate formulations.

An example of both the simplicity and the complexity comes in an anecdote related by a friend. He describes how he excelled in first-year French class because he had a crush on his teacher. Independent of the teaching method, the textbook, the AV materials, or other such apparatus, his participation in life guaranteed his ability to learn and perform. His passion for the teacher sparked a passion for language.

The next year, with a different teacher, his academic career plummeted. It is worth noting that this friend is a native French speaker. His interaction with family and friends had made him fluent long before formal schooling. In school, he extended that fluency into literature, composition, and the more formal study of language. We could itemize the practices that fostered both his language learning both in and out of school, but the difference between years one and two went beyond educational methods. None of his journey fits neatly into a narrative of either systematic instruction or "natural" learning.

The dialogue between Artemis and Athena is pictured in Figure 10.1. Note that their domains overlap, but also that most of the ecosystem of learning lies outside of their technical arguments. The reality of one student's love for a teacher, an elderly person's stress over memory loss, an immigrant's experience of changes in life context, the inspiration of a child from a field science project, the nurturing of a student who had dropped out of school, the reading of a novel (hidden by the large history textbook), and endless other examples shows that any discussion about education is severely limited if it does not take into account the diversity of life and learning.

If we must pick a third incarnation to represent that larger view, it might be *Maia*, the goddess of springtime, warmth, and growth. However, Maia

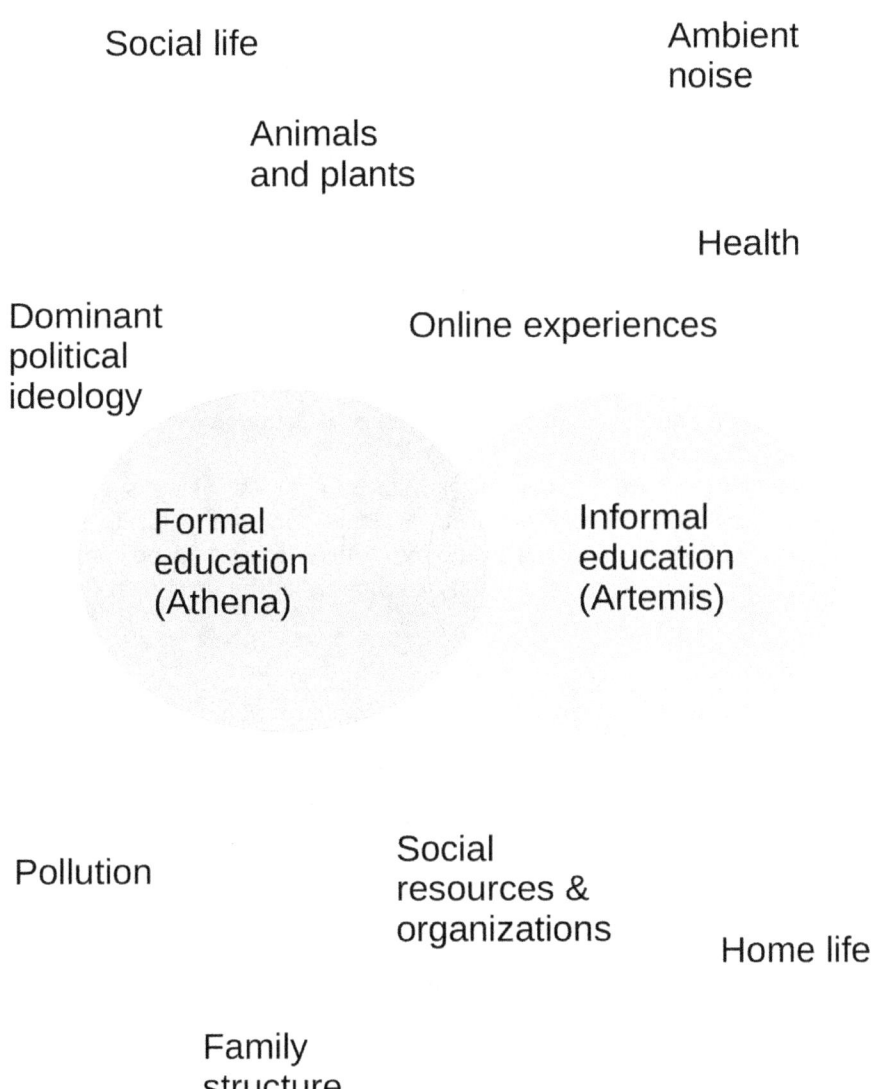

Figure 10.1. Dialogue between Athena and Artemis.

does not offer a third option for delivering education. Instead, she asks us to situate education within the vast array of life. For example, the supply of electricity is a major factor for learning, enabling light for reading and computers, and possibly heat or cooling. The issue of electric or other energy supply is an ever-present characteristic of educational ecosystems even though it is rarely mentioned in discussions of either formal or informal learning.

Maia asks us to use something like the ELF to answer basic pedagogical questions. The goal is to move beyond the either/or dichotomy and articulate the extent and manner in which different modes of learning might benefit from one another. It also helps to address the divide between individualistic goals for education, such as career preparation, and social goals, such as creating a democratic society.

Who Learns (and Who Teaches)?

The technical approach to education obscures how sociopolitical factors determine who is even given the opportunity to learn. It appears that both Athena and Artemis focus on how knowledge is acquired by an individual. But learning is a social process.

Moreover, economic injustice, prejudice, and increasing segregation mean that schooling is very far from its equal opportunity ideal. Schools themselves reflect the political economy of their ecosystem position. The opportunities for students are severely circumscribed by their own communities:

> African-American children from low-income urban families frequently suffer from health problems that lead to school absences; from frequent or sustained parental unemployment that provokes family crises; from rent or mortgage defaults causing household moves that entail changes of teachers and schools, with a resulting loss of instructional continuity; and from living in communities with high levels of crime and disorder, where schools spend more time on discipline and less on instruction and where stress depresses academic success.[3]

If we want to understand who is able to learn in what ways, we need to consider the entire ecosystem for students, parents, and schools.

What Is Learned?

The distinction that Artemis sets forth is not just a question for pedagogy taken narrowly. It has political and moral consequences as well. Richard Shaull frames the contrast starkly:

> There is no such thing as a neutral education process. Education either functions ... to facilitate the integration of generations into the logic of the present system and bring about conformity to it, or it becomes the practice of freedom, the means by which men and women deal critically with reality and discover how to participate in the transformation of their world.[4]

When we examine the various ways that people learn, and the variety of situations that give rise to learning, it is clear that what Freire calls the banking model is inadequate in two major ways. One is that it does not accurately describe how people learn. The teacher cannot simply fill the student's head with ideas. Stripped of significance, the teacher's words become, as Freire says, "hollow, alienated, and alienating verbosity." Second, attempting to teach based on it is likely to be very ineffective, or counterproductive to promoting engaged, self-directed learners.

One could debate the need and value of the Common Core Standards, or the specifics for grade and subject area. It is clear, though, that the project is school oriented, focusing on what schools should do. The standards promote equity in formal education and clarity on achievable goals, both reasonable aims. However, the focus on math and literacy, and even there, just within school, says little about other aspects of learning, especially those that are difficult to assess, such as arts, innovation, civic engagement, or moral development. They say very little about outside-of-school learning, or subjects that are barely taught at all in schools.

Some of the most important learning occurs prior to acquisition of skills and knowledge. The novice in an area needs to learn how, and be allowed, to participate with others. Lave and Wenger use the term *legitimate peripheral participation* for this process. It provides a way to speak about the relations between new and experienced participants in an activity system. Newcomers cannot accomplish complex tasks on their own, but once welcomed into the system, they can observe, ask questions, and assume responsibility for parts of the task. This social process "includes, indeed it subsumes, the learning of knowledgeable skills."[5] The what of learning must include learning how to participate.

The need to learn how to thrive, or just to survive, in diverse ecological niches means that pre-packaged learning is unlikely to have much value. Instead, the learner needs to rely on social skills to join the group, and develop an experimental attitude to cope with new and challenging situations.

The learning ecosystems perspective shifts us from the idea that learning happens in the heads of individuals, placing it instead within social arrangements. In a highly perceptive analysis of a nine-year-old child (Adam) being classified as learning disabled, Ray McDermott makes a similar argument.

Adam was labeled as learning disabled. This led to a search for causes and remedies applicable across all settings. Through a detailed ethnographic study, McDermott found that Adam's "disability" depended on how much his performance was subject to degradation in different settings. For example, Adam was constructed as learning disabled the most during testing sessions, less so in classroom lessons, less still in Cooking Club, and least in everyday life.

McDermott concludes that the social conditions of learning, whether in school or daily life, define which pieces of information are relevant: "Learning does not belong to individual persons, but to the various conversations of which they are a part."[6] He does allow that some children for a variety of reasons learn much slower or in different ways than others in some settings. However, it is social arrangements that make something of these differential rates of learning. Learning disability does not exist as a context-free condition.

Where Does Learning Occur?

Illich asks us to consider failures of schooling and the harmful effects of its successes. Formal lessons can be devoid of meaningful opportunities for students to develop social responsibility and a moral compass. A broader definition of education includes the set of practices and experiences that have a formative impact on an individual. This allows for informal education, such as might occur in a museum, online, or through work and play. Students then may ignite their fire of learning based on ordinary life experiences as well as on what a teacher says.

However, complete de-schooling may not be the answer. Learning is enhanced by the relations between learning spaces. For example, when learning is viewed as a lifelong activity, which is not limited to the school, that same school can become a place to reflect upon and extend experiences from work or play. Museums and libraries can become bridges between ordinary experiences and more formalized learning in classrooms. Comparing experiences across spaces is an opportunity for critique, for example, experiencing a museum exhibit that provides a different perspective on another culture than one has garnered on the playground.

Going further, we can see that learning develops most fully not only in binary relations between learning spaces but also in a richly connected network of learning spaces. In a recent study of transcontextual writing by young men, Anna Smith shows how important this can be for writing and personal development. Participants in her study negotiated identities across contexts, influencing how they both adopted and resisted specific writing practices.[7]

When Does Learning Occur?

Learning occurs all the time, although we may not recognize it as such. In his essay "On Listening," Plutarch quotes the fourth-century professor Libanius, who describes the behavior of his students:

> some arriving late; some constantly signaling and passing messages about other more exciting matters; some standing and posing like statues with arms

crossed, or picking their noses; others sitting in the general confusion, or forcibly holding down the more enthusiastic; some alleviating their boredom by counting newcomers, staring blankly out of the window or gossiping with a neighbour; some applauding inanely; or finally stamping out, drawing others in their trail.[8]

For Libanius's students, their messages concerned "more exciting matters" than those in his lectures. This happens through messages, gossiping, even staring out the window. We can concur with Libanius that their behavior is inappropriate, but we cannot say that learning is not occurring.

There are different ways to frame learning. Rather than seeking the one solution, we ought to consider the variety of ways that people actually learn and how they interconnect.

Why Do People Learn?

There are many goals for education, some stated with reference to the individual and some for society as a whole (see chapter 4). Progressive educators of the twentieth century brought these together in their goal of developing "critical, socially engaged intelligence, which enables individuals to understand and participate effectively in the affairs of their community in a collaborative effort to achieve a common good."[9]

This means human flourishing, a common translation for the Greek term *eudaimonia*. Eudaimonia refers to an objective state characterizing the well-lived life, not simply a transient or subjective feeling of pleasure. According to Aristotle, flourishing means exercising reason, as the soul's most proper and nourishing activity. His idea of reason is closely related to a sense of wholeness, integrated with emotion, development of aesthetic sensibility, and morality, as much as to intellectual development. Eudaimonia is usually defined as a characteristic of how one lives in relation to others. It is thus a social ethical condition, not just an individual or personal state.

Aspects of the progressive vision for the good life can be seen in President Johnson's speech inaugurating the Great Society. It is a place where every child can learn and develop talents. "Leisure is a welcome chance to build and reflect, not a feared cause of boredom and restlessness.... The city of [humanity] serves not only the needs of the body and the demands of commerce but the desire for beauty and the hunger for community."[10] Johnson's failure to end the U.S. war in Vietnam was, of course, a denial of the very good life he invoked and became a barrier to creating the Great Society. It is all the more striking that his call is so discordant with the dominant education discourse today, which places little value on leisure, beauty, or community.

How Do People Learn?

A metaphor that contrasts with the systematic instillation of knowledge, according more with constructivism, is Deleuze and Guattari's idea of *rhizomatic knowledge*. It implies that learning is most effective when it allows participants to adapt to continually evolving circumstances, including the definition of the task.

Rhizomatic learning emphasizes student involvement, in contrast to conventional models of pedagogy, in which the teacher defines the learning task, its methods, and its evaluation. It has also been described as a model for the community as curriculum and for net-enabled education.

Dave Cormier provides a useful summary:

> In the rhizomatic model of learning, curriculum is not driven by predefined inputs from experts; it is constructed and negotiated in real time by the contributions of those engaged in the learning process. This community acts as the curriculum, spontaneously shaping, constructing, and reconstructing itself and the subject of its learning in the same way that the rhizome responds to changing environmental conditions.[11]

The metaphor of rhizomatic learning has been applied across many areas of pedagogy. It is inherently a social view of learning and knowledge, which leads to ideas such as crowdsourcing the curriculum. This implies inclusion of open resources via a peer-generated approach, in contrast to a course designer carefully selecting a small set of canonical readings. This is a good example of student construction of a learning niche.[12]

How Does Education Prepare Us for Life?

Education occurs in a wide variety of settings with varying degrees of intentionality. A familiar trope describes two starkly different models of learning.

In the first, learning is organic and nonhierarchical. Conversation, rather than lecture, is the dominant form of discourse. Learning is hands on, collaborative, and purposeful. This type of learning is sometimes attributed to traditional learning in agrarian societies, in which learning is driven by situation, such as accomplishing the planting or harvesting needed that day. Alternatively, it is assumed to occur outside of the contemporary classroom through children's play, mundane community activities, work and apprenticeships, or organizations such as 4-H clubs and nature centers. Learning in this model comes by means of activity rather than as a prerequisite for it, such as Artemis would prefer.

One could describe this model as emphasizing learning and Athena's banking model as emphasizing teaching. Although such a distinction can be a useful starting point, especially when it encourages us to imagine different forms of pedagogy, it is limiting when examined more closely. Regardless of the framing, it is difficult to find pure examples of pedagogy in practice that cleanly reveal organic versus mechanistic, agrarian versus industrial, or banking versus practice-of-freedom pedagogy. The very fact that we find ourselves wrestling with the dichotomy is due to the influence of Athena's model.

The advent of modern, industrial society did not in any sense eliminate situated learning. At the same time, agrarian or traditional learning is often more hierarchical and directive than the modern academy. Moreover, much of the learning that actually occurs in the modern classroom is informal, conversational, and situation based.

Informal, conversational, and situation-based learning characterizes what many students spend most of their time actually doing in school, regardless of the official curriculum. In an ethnographic study of high school, Penelope Eckert found that social tracking, seen in groups such as "jocks" and "burnouts," was a major determinant of students' experiences in school.

They operate within opposed class cultures, which emerge from an interaction among different existing social classes outside of school, the school's institutional environment, and allegiances among the students themselves. The cultures in turn serve as a social tracking system. These dynamics define student experiences and learning more than any details of the mandated curriculum.[13]

In that case, the learning may be about social media, fashion, cliques, or sports, as Eckert found, rather than the concepts of the formal curriculum, but speaking descriptively, rather than normatively, it is what students do.

At the same time, learning in so-called informal settings is often more didactic and teacher driven than anything typically found in schools. Consider, for example, members of a religious organization, a scout group, or a club being told to memorize a creed, or to carry out ritualized practices that are not to be questioned.

The traditional/modern distinction does not reflect the permeable boundaries of social organizations. Even the most locked-down urban school with a high wall around it is infused with community influences, as can be seen in Eckert's study. The problem is not only that a banking model of education discourages creativity and independent thinking. It is simply not possible to download knowledge; all learning is inquiry-based learning.

How Do We Measure Success?

One of the best program evaluation studies ever conducted was the Eight-Year Study of progressive education conducted between 1932 and 1940.[14] Thirty high schools participated. The students from the experimental schools did only slightly better on standardized test scores, but they showed major improvement in other areas, including thinking skills; work habits and study skills; appreciation of music, art, literature, and other aesthetic experiences; social attitudes and social sensitivity; personal-social adjustment; philosophy of life; and physical fitness. Students from the most progressive schools showed the most improvement, more than those in the somewhat progressive schools, and much more than those in traditional schools. There was evidence of long-term impact as well.

The progressive schools realized that few parents or citizens would be satisfied if children could successfully answer multiple-choice questions requiring narrowly focused skills but failed to develop intellectual curiosity, cultural awareness, practical skills, a healthy philosophy of life, a strong moral character, emotional balance, social fitness, sensitivity to social problems, or physical fitness. Instead of narrowly defined subjects, the curriculum used broad themes of significance to the students, which would start with life as the students experienced it. Students would engage in inquiry as a way to make sense of themselves and the world around them.

How Should Schools Relate to the Outside World?

Educators have increasingly seen the value of building a healthy learning community in the classroom and school, especially as they emphasize teaching social and emotional skills, and incorporate methods such as dialogue, collaboration, and project-based learning. These communities require diversity and a commitment to learning how to learn.

At the college level, a variety of curricular structures have been developed to link together existing courses, or even to restructure the entire curriculum, so that students "have opportunities for deeper understanding and integration of the material they are learning, and more interaction with one another and their teachers as fellow participants in the learning enterprise."[15] Learning communities are intended to foster *integrative learning*, "students' abilities to integrate learning—over time, across courses, and between academic, personal, and community life."[16]

The ultimate goal of learning communities is not just to enact learning more effectively, but to practice democracy within formal education. This entails schools implementing democratic education on a day-to-day basis. We then expect to see practices such as self-directed learning, shared decision making, individualized project-based work, and student-chosen internships in the community. Working for democratic learning and for a democratic society become one.[17]

In learning communities, educators creatively engage learners, providing them with choice in their learning. Youth voices are encouraged through forums such as student councils, committees, and clubs. Students have the opportunity to contribute to educational planning and decision making in a context where their input is routinely muted, if not altogether absent.

Education can serve as a corrective when a community, or the larger society, veers off course. If a community becomes chaotic, or appears to lose its grounding, education can remind it of traditional values and long-term trends. When the community becomes stagnant, holding on to dysfunctional ideas from earlier times, or lacking needed innovation, education can become the instigator of change. Postman describes this countervailing function of education as thermostatic: Education conserves tradition when the rest of the environment is innovative, or it is innovative when the rest of the society is tradition bound.[18]

Postman's thermostat has a simple, binary relationship to a heating system. It flips the system on when the air is cold and flips it off when the air is warm enough. That captures the notion of balance in ecology. In an analogous way by standing apart from the larger ecosystem, the education thermostat can keep it in balance.

There is an appeal in the notion of a wise parental-type figure watching over and correcting society's volatility (or stagnation). But in order to achieve the balancing function that Postman advocates, schools need to be independent of the rest of the social, cultural, and natural environments. Although the thermostat is useful, a deeper connection can more fully enrich education and its role in society.

A model for that deeper connection appears in the technique now known as "management by wandering around." Abraham Lincoln was an early practitioner of this idea (though not the term). He would informally inspect Union army troops in the early part of the Civil War. Through random appearances, he could improve morale, productivity, and a sense of purpose, especially as compared to waiting for reports, which might never come, or issuing directives that made little sense in context.[19] Lincoln knew that he could not stand apart from the ecosystem and direct it from afar as a thermostat might do. We could think of other such relations between education and daily life as different types of organizational collaboration, varying from total independence through strategic alliance to networking.

What Is the Role of Literacy?

Learning derives from our participation in the world, usually through some form of community, whether in the family and neighborhood, the workplace, or leisure activities. It is only in the modern era, especially in the twentieth century, that we have successfully divorced much of learning from daily life, by means of formal education, textbooks, curriculum guides, testing, certifications, and ironically through the supposedly revolutionary new information and communication technologies.

Early studies of educational software showed a parallel to problem-posing versus banking education. Unexpected problems were more motivating and more conducive to learning than carefully crafted lessons. In one case, a program designed to teach specific arithmetic skills had a bug in it, so it was actually mis-teaching. Users began to play with it to discover how the bug worked and what might account for its behavior. In so doing, they became even more engaged in learning, and their mathematical knowledge was challenged and extended.

Teachers in that same study examined various examples of software. They described general software tools with which students could explore their own questions as "flexible, engaging, interactive, nonjudgmental, clear, graphic, dramatic." They "saw the enormous pedagogical difference between solving problems and formulating them, between answering someone else's question and generating your own."[20]

Everyday life experience, especially problems, such as the software bug, has educative potential. However, experience alone is not enough. We must make sense of the experience in light of other experiences we have had.

How Can We Learn Abstract Ideas?

There is utility in breaking things apart and simplifying the complexity of the concrete. We could never account in detail for all the factors that contribute to the exact manner in which a single leaf falls. We progress in understanding by working with models of wind currents or properties of materials. The postulation of underlying principles or constituent elements, such as atoms, has proven enormously useful for science, and for learning. Combining a holistic approach with an atomistic one can help us understand any complex phenomenon.

Beyond these epistemological considerations, there are psychological justifications for needing a time to experience and a time to remember, a time for action and time for reflection, a time for doing and time for talking. Reports of immediate experience contrast with those of past episodes, which depend on accurate retrieval of feelings and integration of experiences over time. Daniel Kahneman describes this as our having an experiencing self and a remembering self.[21]

These arguments apply to any kind of learning. But consider just one example. When we learn a new language, we benefit greatly from having opportunities to employ it freely, especially in circumstances where we do not have time to think about what we are doing. For example, in a shop in a foreign country, we might ask about the location of a product, its features, or its cost, without stopping to consider precise rules of pronunciation or grammar. We simply want to accomplish the task, and find ourselves improving our fluency through unconscious imitation and interaction. Most people find that there is no substitute for that kind of direct experience with native speakers.

At other times, systematic study of the regularities and exceptions of grammar, the nuances of meaning as found in a dictionary, and historical and regional variations of the language can be essential. Direct experience is important. It gives us a facility with situated language use in that one shop, but it inevitably omits vast realms of language use, leaving us ill prepared for, say, discussing local politics or reading an academic journal in that language.

The renowned mathematician Edward Frenkel hated math in school, as many people do. He was far more interested in physics, with its promise of understanding the fundamental nature of the universe. But he changed after his mentoring by a math professor, who listened to Frenkel's questions and showed him aspects of math that he would never have encountered in school, or in any well-ordered curriculum of math concepts. Frenkel writes:

> When I was growing up, I wasn't aware of the hidden world of mathematics. Like most people, I thought math was a stale, boring subject. But I was lucky in my last year of high school. I met a professional mathematician who opened the magical world of math to me. I learned that mathematics is full of infinite possibilities as well as elegance and beauty, just like poetry, art, and music. I fell in love with math.[22]

Frenkel came to love mathematics because of the people around him, including two mentors and his parents; because of his earlier passion for physics; and perhaps in part because of his feeling that it was a hidden world, previously inaccessible to him. This was ecosystem-based learning. (A fuller discussion would consider the impact of the anti-Semitism of Russia in the 1980s on his education.)

Of all the mythologies that we live by one of the most pernicious is that we can fully understand a subject such as mathematics, break it into small bits and pieces, and then teach it in an orderly fashion. We compound the error by thinking that with enough effort we can make the subject engaging for most, if not all, students, while systematically ignoring their own interests and questions. Doing so not only fails in the ostensible purpose of transmitting the bits and pieces of mathematics; it misses the opportunity to enable the love that Frenkel discovered. Both his case and that of the ordinary math-hating student tell us that that the transmission myth is false.

Should the Community Be the Curriculum?

Accepting the community as curriculum means that we open the doors of the classroom. Moreover, we abandon the goal of "covering." David Hawkins contends, "You don't want to cover a subject; you want to uncover it."[23] If learning is truly open to the world, the teacher doesn't have to, cannot, know it all. Instead, she or he becomes a fellow explorer, possibly a knowledgeable guide, but not the final answer to anything.

But at the very least, the project of building community must be coupled with awareness of the negative aspects of education ecosystems. In particular, many youth of color encounter racism, sexism, and homophobia, often coping with these in isolation. They suffer discriminatory policing and sentencing practices, replicated by detention and suspensions within school. Limited educational opportunities and low wages restrict economic opportunities. A *social ecology* perspective reveals these social, political, and economic forces within communities and in the larger society that influence the youth development.[24]

PARTIAL CONCEPTIONS OF EDUCATION ECOSYSTEMS

The term *education ecosystem* is often used to refer to the system *within* an organization, such as a school, a university program, or a corporate office. When extraorganizational factors are included, they are typically seen only as factors impacting the ecosystem per se. For example, one might talk about how affluent parents take their children to theater and museums, or summer science programs, and that those experiences enhance the success of those children in school, as well as the equity of schooling overall. But the analysis is often just from the outside in, how those outside phenomena influence performance of the school.

A second, important use of the term is to talk about new technologies for learning, such as social media, online resources, and learning management systems. For example, the incorporation of Wikipedia reading and writing into curricula opens up paths to learning that go far beyond the usual prepared textbooks, and other educational materials:

> We believe Wikipedia and its sister projects belong in education. When students of all ages contribute to Wikimedia projects as part of their learning, they gain significant twenty-first century skills. By fostering a relationship between Education and the Wikimedia movement, we have the best chance to realize our goal that the sum of all knowledge will be accessible to everyone in the world for free.[25]

Some advocates for new media in education focus on how new tools can enrich the classroom. Others ignore the classroom and focus on online experiences per se.

A third application of the term is for a corporate learning ecosystem. Here, the goal is to enhance workplace learning. The ecosystem formulation allows managers to talk about a single system comprising on-the-job learning and formal training.

FULL ECOSYSTEM PERSPECTIVE

A full ecosystem perspective positions learning as occurring in all aspects of life. It reveals the many, diverse ways that we learn and how different media, modes, and venues for learning synergistically promote growth. These various learning opportunities complement and amplify one another and may occasionally contradict. From this perspective, the connections among learning experiences become as salient as any individual experience. Properties of the system as a whole emerge, properties that make learning and life inseparable.

Consider just one aspect of the overall education ecosystem, the relation between formal schooling and community life (see Figure 10.2). We can use ecological analysis to explore how

- life in schools works as a microcosm of life in the community,
- life in the community works as a macrocosm of life in the school,
- learning within schools shapes community life, and
- learning within the community shapes the schools.

This analysis would show various ways that *community* can relate to learning: We can learn inside school, with that enhanced perhaps by a vibrant

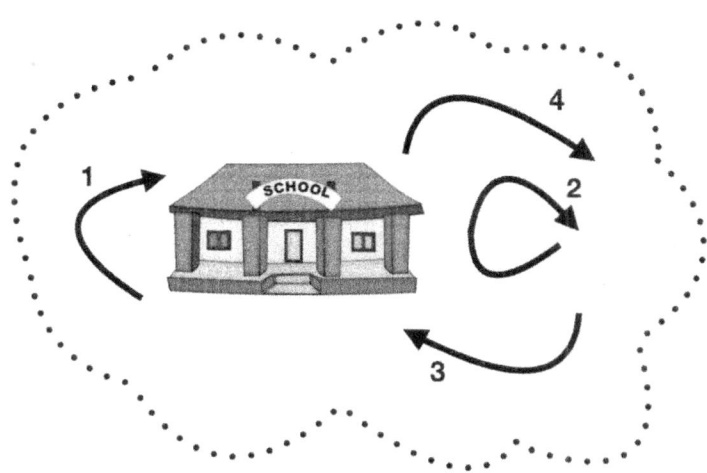

Figure 10.2. Pedagogical Relations between School and Community.

learning community. We learn through the community per se, as in the bahal. We can learn from inside to outside, by the school connecting with and transforming community. And we can learn from outside to inside, drawing from funds of knowledge in the community.

Conceiving a student not as a repository for inert facts but as a living organism in an ecosystem leads us to think of every educational issue in a different way. For example, musical training is usually considered as a fine thing to do, but not central to the educational mission, certainly less so than STEM, even when that acronym is expanded to STEAM.

Yet a growing body of research shows the contribution of musical experience to areas such as auditory and spatial perception, and literacy skills. In the brain, significant structural differences develop in the precentral gyri, the corpus callosum, and the auditory cortex. Moreover, musical understanding plays a critical role in history and cultural studies and opens up major aspects of science.

Music is a well-recognized part of healthy human experience. The point is not that it ought to be added as another essential skill to be taught, but that if one begins with the idea that education should promote full human growth, music is there from the beginning, automatically part of education's ecosystem. It plays in students' earbuds, in streaming media, and in the way we move. It is tragic that formal music education seems to be dropped automatically in any funding crisis, but music itself is still part of the ecosystem.

The network shown in Figure 10.2 is just part of the overall education ecosystem. Analytically, we need to understand better the many direct and indirect aspects of that system. Programmatically, we need to begin with the systems view and not simply add on to historically established forms of pedagogy.

ECOPEDAGOGY

What would it mean to teach with full appreciation of education's ecosystem? What would an *Ecosystem Curriculum* look like? It is important to say first that this does not mean a curriculum to teach all about ecosystems. That would be an important project, one that intersects in important ways, but it is not the same. Instead, *Ecosystem Curriculum* here means the intentional application of an understanding of the ecosystem of learning in the organization of learning, teaching, mentoring, materials, facilities, assessment, certification, and all other aspects of formal and informal education.

At a system level, the ecosystems perspective seeks to understand and nurture a healthy environment for learning with diverse, interacting components. Formal schooling is an important part of that, but it is not the only locus. Libraries, museums, community centers, homes, sports clubs, music and arts, the Internet, friends and family, homes, natural habitats, workplaces, farms, playgrounds, health centers, summer camps, day care centers, houses of worship, retirement homes, clubs, and more are part of that environment.

Learning through inquiry occurs in each of these settings. These learning spaces each offer affordances for different topics and purposes, but can each contribute to holistic growth. They are sites for participation, colloquium, and transformation, not simply places to apply learning or alternative ways to learn. Connections among these are much less understood than are the individual pieces, yet it is through the connections that the greatest learning and growth often occur.

The ecosystem of education needs to be nurtured, just as does an individual biological organism or an entire biological ecosystem. That nurturing requires not making schools more efficient, but making them more relevant to the unrealized potentials of ordinary life. Community inside the school needs to be connected to learning in communities outside the school and to its cultural-historical meanings. Without these connections, the learning ecosystem fails to thrive. It also falls short of its potential to provide both stability and challenge to the larger society and, in particular, to the possibilities for democratic life.

Ecopedagogy is a movement to develop *planetary citizens* to respect and take action for all life. It asks how we can participate in the creation of a healthy, resilient, and nourishing world. This calls for inclusive education, which engages the current social and ecological crisis, and encourages people to become critical, socially engaged citizens.[26] Ecopedagogy cannot be about single issues, much less inert ideas disconnected from each other and from use. As Audre Lorde says, "There is no such thing as a single-issue struggle because we do not live single-issue lives."[27]

No issue demands a system-level understanding more than the climate disruption we all face. Climate science seems to consistently underestimate the severity of the situation. The largest uncertainty is not in the climate science per se, but in how humans will respond.[28] Education cannot guarantee that we will have even a partially adequate response to climate change. However, basing pedagogy on a view of learners as whole individuals with moral, physical, and mental aspects and knowledge as a connected web of ideas offers hope for people who can respond in a healthy way. This is but one of many examples in which the health of the biologic ecosystem and the learning ecosystem are interdependent.

SOME GUIDELINES

The five principles for education ecosystems offer a useful starting point for thinking about a generative ecosystem curriculum:

1. Diversity of organisms and learning niches
2. Network of interactions among components
3. Emergence of new properties, not predictable from the parts
4. Finding and constructing learning niches
5. Interpretation of the environment

1. Diversity of Organisms and Learning Niches

The first principle suggests that learning proceeds best when there are opportunities to participate in multiple environments, offering diverse challenges and multiple perspectives on knowledge. Learning takes place throughout life in all sorts of situations, in and out of school. Moreover, different learners benefit from different media and approaches to pedagogy, different learning niches. Among other things, this calls for an expanded conception of learning by doing.

For example, work can be a powerful force for learning and is thus a key aspect of education's ecosystem. We should treat the knowledge gained through work as legitimate for academic growth as well as for job preparation. This does not mean simply certifying so many hours spent, but developing ways in which students can reflect on their work experience in terms of practical knowledge, links to the experiences of others, connections to theory, community values, and personal development.

Similarly, the natural world should be more than an afterthought, such as an occasional field trip, or a topic to explore through videos and simulations on the Web. Instead, direct observation and interaction should be essential parts of learning. Moreover, we should not only learn *about* nature, but also *from* nature. Robin Kimmerer writes that

> in Native ways of knowing . . . humans have the least experience with how to live and thus the most to learn—we must look to our teachers among the other species for guidance. Their wisdom is apparent in the way that they live. They teach us by example. . . . I used to teach just the way I was taught, but now I let someone else do all the work for me. If plants are our oldest teachers, why not let them teach?[29]

An organization for formal learning (school, university, hospital, training center, etc.) can become the social center of the community. Then, success of the community becomes a more valid indicator of the success of learning than decontextualized standardized tests. Specific measures might include levels and quality of employment, health, housing, and community engagement. The idea of community success needs to be examined critically, of course. There are multiple levels of community in which we participate, from the local neighborhood to the global, and the sense of community may be quite different in a small village or a large city.

2. Network of Interactions among Components

The relations among different venues for learning may be more significant than what takes places within one of them. We may, for example, collaborate on a community improvement project that uses new media and includes direct engagement with nature. Engaging with a natural habitat in a direct physical way, then exploring its properties through simulations and visualizations, and applying the knowledge gained for social purposes can lead to richer, more integrated, deeper, and lasting learning.

A commonly held view is that information and communications technologies are tools that will automatically improve education. This view sprouts from the belief that technology and social practices are in separate realms, that the technology is autonomous, something to be found in a metal box or in code for accomplishing a specific task.

However, technology in use is an interacting network of people, texts, artifacts, activities, ideology, and cultural meanings, in short, an ecosystem of its own. That system does not improve, speed up, or determine social practices from the outside. Instead it becomes new social practices or integrates with existing ones.[30] This means that we need to consider the overarching system implied by a technology and work with that in the design of curricula and teaching. When we do that, we see the enormous potential of new social practices to expand, even unbind, the colloquium of the school.

3. Emergence of New Properties, Not Predictable from the Parts

One problem with organizing learning around life activities is that they may not cooperate with specific learning objectives. There can be bureaucratic obstacles or vagaries of weather. And not everyone is interested in the same life activities or has the same values relative to those.

But the biggest problem concerns purpose. If the pedagogical goal is to instill a particular skill or bit of knowledge, it is usually more efficient to do that directly, and not count on a rich lived experience to magically bring it to fruition. If, on the other hand, the goal is to foster the ability to thrive in the face of complexity and uncertainty, as one encounters in all of life, then avoiding that life experience will not help.

The science educator Jack Easley had been working in a second grade class guiding a six-week-long unit on weather. Pupils learned about clouds, precipitation, storms, weather measurement, agriculture, and other such important topics, taught no doubt in an engaging way. On the last day, it was raining outside until just before the class ended. Jack knew that there might be a rainbow. Viewing that could be an exciting culmination for the unit.

He took the class outside, preparing to discuss the visible light spectrum, refraction, moisture in air, and other such topics. But the pupils weren't interested. While Jack was looking up, they were looking down at the closer and more ordinary. He was a latter-day Thales at risk of falling into a well while gazing at the stars. The children's observations of the worms led them to ask, "Why do worms come out of the ground after a rain?"

Jack started to answer, then realized that he did not know. So he asked the students to write down their question for scientists at the university. It turned out that those scientists had many theories, but they did not really know, either. This is a vital question for agriculture, but the answer is not simple. Even today, the scientific questions are not fully answered.

The phenomenon of the worms rising from the ground is itself an emergent property of a system comprising the worms, soil, nutrients, rain, terrain, air and land temperatures, and more. Pedagogically it is an emergent property of the weather unit, including Jack's willingness to take the children outside.

If the curricular goal of teaching about weather per se, or about rainbows, were paramount, we might deem the worm diversion to be a failure. Although loosely coupled to the material, it stole precious time from the curriculum unit as originally conceived. But if the goal were to engage students in scientific inquiry, building on the excitement from their own question was exactly the right thing to do.

4. Finding and Constructing Learning Niches

Academic learning should be a complement to life in the community, learning from it and returning value to it. Writing projects, for example, can be designed to effect change in the community, document progress, inform or inspire community members, or highlight problems.[31] Community asset maps can help citizens understand better their own resources and challenges. Some college and university programs now focus on engaging young adults in community decision making.[32] In these ways, learners not only participate in their environments and are shaped by them; they also help to create or re-create them. Jane Addams calls this new vision making "the entire social organism democratic," extending "democracy beyond its political expression."[33]

5. Interpretation of the Environment

The standard model for education is some kind of colloquium, and that in fact is how many would define "education," as distinct from "learning." Unfortunately, the formal colloquium often reduces to talk by the teacher alone coupled with a predefined set of reading materials. It may expand to include talk by students and materials more responsive to their backgrounds, interests, and questions.

Dialogue with books, teachers, other students, family, and so on is essential, even though it rarely develops in a predictable, linear fashion. The nature of the learning community, both within the school and in the ecosystem comprising the school and other elements of society, is vital, both to what can be learned and as a subject to understand per se.

It is also evident that schools are embedded in the surrounding society; they perpetuate the social relations that define that society. Formal schooling is interpreted by learners in the context of its time and place in their society. A consequence is that schooling often fails to take advantage of the diversity of learning in the world beyond the local.

RECONCEIVING LEARNING

These principles lead to a reconception of how we learn, both in and out of school. They are essentially stances that we take toward complex situations and challenging problems. For example, by communicating through multiple media, we can learn from contemporaries, but also from the accumulated wisdom represented in culture and disciplinary knowledge. Alternatively, one could engage more directly with nature for a less mediated experience. However, no form of learning can be totally unmediated. Even a walk in the woods is shaped by the paths that others have made.

One might well ask whether this exercise simply replaces one way of carving up learning (by subject areas and grade levels) with another, learning spaces versus learning topics. A transdisciplinary perspective envisions both topics and spaces, with inquiry organizing activity and learning. The inquiry may be into an academic question, a community-based problem, a personal reflection, an aesthetic challenge, or any of a variety of other questions seen as meaningful by the participants.

The aim is to bring experiences, beliefs, values, and problems from the world into reflective inquiry, and to carry new knowledge to apply in life. The school can then become an organic whole, and part of larger ecosystem wholes. Learning is part and parcel of our life on this one earth:

> All studies arise from aspects of the one earth and the one life lived upon it. We do not have a series of stratified earths, one of which is mathematical,

another physical, another historical, and so on. . . . All studies grow out of relations in the one great common world. When the child lives in varied but concrete and active relationship to this common world, his studies are naturally unified. . . . Relate the school to life, and all studies are of necessity correlated.[34]

SUMMARY

Some educators have ignored the call for integrated learning, whether as Dewey formulated it above, or as promoted by Célestin Freinet, bell hooks, neo-Confucians, the Carnegie Foundation, or many others. The dominant forces in the education system have, if anything, moved toward more piecemeal, easily tested knowledge acquisition. Those forces typically consign schools to preparing workers for capitalist production, and show little concern for purposes such as developing civic intelligence or developing the full human potential.

However, many other educators in the United States and around the world have tried hard to teach in an integrated way, crisscrossing disciplines and linking school and society. We need to locate the successes, even partial ones, and seek to understand how they have done it. We also need to do a better job of explaining why so many efforts have fallen short. Perhaps a more explicit ecological understanding can help in those endeavors.

A pessimist might say at this point that even a highly perceptive ecological understanding must still face the test of responding to the forces that have reduced modern education to a factory process. Any substantive change in education depends on the larger project of educating the citizenry as a whole not only to accept, but to demand a system that nutures students develop critical awareness, holistic understanding, and the ability to work together for democratic life.

NOTES

1. Haeckel coined the word *ecology* in 1866. This passage is quoted in Robert C. Stauffer, "Haeckel, Darwin, and Ecology," *The Quarterly Review of Biology* 32, no. 2 (June 1957): 138–44: 140.

2. Bertram C. Bruce and Maureen P. Hogan, "The Disappearance of Technology: Toward an Ecological Model of Literacy," in *Handbook of Literacy and Technology: Transformations in a Post-Typographic World*, ed. David Reinking, Michael C. McKenna, Linda D. Labbo, and Ronald D. Kieffer (Florence, KY: Routledge, 1998), 269–81; Paul Emerich France, "A Healthy Ecosystem for Classroom Management," *Educational Leadership* 76, no. 1 (September 2018); William Timberlake, "An Ecological Approach to Learning," *Learning and Motivation* 15, no. 4 (November 1984): 321–33; Todd Kern and Adam Rubin, *Designing the Future of Learning* (New York: 2Revolutions, 2012); Katherine Prince, "Innovating toward a Vibrant Learning Ecosystem: Ten Pathways for Transforming Learning," KnowledgeWorks, accessed January 20, 2020, https://knowledgeworks.org/wp-content/uploads/2018/01/innovation-pathways-transforming-learning.pdf.

3. Richard Rothstein and Mark Santow, "A Different Kind of Choice: Educational Inequality and the Continuing Significance of Racial Segregation," Working Paper, Economic Policy Institute, August 21, 2012, 1.

4. Richard Shaull, "Foreword," in *Paulo Freire, Pedagogy of the Oppressed* (New York: Continuum, 1970), 15.

5. Jean Lave and Etienne Wenger, *Situated Learning: Legitimate Peripheral Participation* (New York: Cambridge University Press, 1991), 29.

6. "The Acquisition of a Child by a Learning Disability," in *Understanding Practice: Perspectives on Activity and Context*, ed. Seth Chailklin and Jean Lave (New York: Cambridge University Press, 1993), 292.

7. Anna Marie Smith, *Transcontextual Writing Development among Young Men* (New York: New York University, 2014).

8. Plutarch, *Essays*, trans. Robin Waterfield (New York: Penguin Classics, 1992), 19.

9. John Dewey Project on Progressive Education, "A Brief Overview of Progressive Education," January 30, 2002.

10. Lyndon B. Johnson, May 22, 1964, remarks at the University of Michigan.

11. Dave Cormier, "Rhizomatic Education: Community as Curriculum," *Innovate: Journal of Online Education* 4, no. 5 (2008).

12. Drew Paulin and Caroline Haythornthwaite, "Crowdsourcing the Curriculum: Redefining E-Learning Practices through Peer-Generated Approaches," *The Information Society* 32, no. 2 (2016): 130–42.

13. Penelope Eckert, *Jocks and Burnouts: Social Categories and Identity in the High School* (New York: Teachers College Press, 1989).

14. Wilford M. Aikin, *The Story of the Eight-Year Study* (New York: Harper, 1942).

15. Faith Gabelnick et al., *Learning Communities: Creating Connections among Students, Faculty, and Disciplines* (San Francisco: Jossey-Bass, 1990), 19.

16. Gerald Lee Ratliff, "Integrative Learning: Opportunities to Connect," January 2007, https://files.eric.ed.gov/fulltext/ED499398.pdf.

17. Pete Pattisson, *How Schools Un-Educate Children* (London, UK: Deptford Green School and Blackfen School for Girls, 2012).

18. Neil Postman, *Teaching as a Conserving Activity* (New York: Delacorte, 1979), 86.

19. Stephen B. Oates, *With Malice toward None: The Life of Abraham Lincoln* (New York: Harper & Row, 1977).

20. Henry F. Olds, Judah L. Schwartz, and Nancy A. Willie, *People and Computers: Who Teaches Whom?* (Newton, MA: Education Development Center, 1980), 40.

21. The general phenomenon was first presented by Kahneman and Jason Riis, in "Living, and Thinking about It: Two Perspectives on Life," in *The Science of Well-Being*, ed. F. A. Huppert, N. Baylis, and B. Keverne (Oxford, UK: Oxford University Press, 2005), 285–304.

22. Edward Frenkel, *Love and Math: The Heart of Hidden Reality* (New York: Basic Books, 2013), 2–3.

23. Quoted by Eleanor Duckworth, *The Having of Wonderful Ideas and Other Essays on Teaching and Learning* (New York: Teachers College Press, 1986), 7.

24. Shawn Ginwright and Taj James, "From Assets to Agents of Change: Social Justice, Organizing, and Youth Development," *New Directions for Youth Development* 96 (Winter 2002): 29.

25. Wikimedia Education Team, "Wikimedia Education," accessed September 2, 2019, https://outreach.wikimedia.org/wiki/Education.

26. Emerging from the work of Paulo Freire, Francisco Gutierrez, Cruz Prado, Greg Misiaszek, and others.

27. Audre Lorde, "Learning from the 60s" (February 1982), para. 14, https://www.blackpast.org/african-american-history/1982-audre-lorde-learning-60s/.

28. David Wallace-Wells, *The Uninhabitable Earth: Life after Warming* (New York: Penguin Random House, 2019).

29. Robin Wall Kimmerer, *Braiding Sweetgrass: Indigenous Wisdom, Scientific Knowledge, and the Teachings of Plants* (Minneapolis, MN: Milkweed Editions, 2013), 9, 232.

30. Bertram C. Bruce, "Technology as Social Practice," *Educational Foundations* 10, no. 4 (Fall 1996): 51–58.

31. Chris Benson and Scott Christian, *Writing to Make a Difference: Classroom Projects for Community Change* (New York: Teachers College Press, 2002).

32. Lee Benson, John Puckett, and Ira Harkavy, *Dewey's Dream: Universities and Democracies in an Age of Education Reform* (Philadelphia: Temple University Press, 2007).

33. "The Subjective Necessity for Social Settlements," in *Philanthropy and Social Progress* (New York: Thomas Y. Crowell & Co., 1893), 2.

34. John Dewey, "The School and Society," MW 1:54–55.

Conclusion

> We cannot seek achievement for ourselves and forget about progress and prosperity for our community. . . . Our ambitions must be broad enough to include the aspirations and needs of others, for their sakes and our own.
> —Cesar Chavez[1]

We know that context makes an enormous difference for learning. A student who is hungry, or who attends a school without books or computers, or has no school at all does not have the same opportunity to learn as one who attends a well-endowed school on a full stomach with ample support from home.

Many of the critiques of education refer to the context as much as to pedagogy in a narrow sense. In some cases they are critiques of the relationship between learning spaces, for example, of how formal classroom and on-the-job learning ought to connect. The contention here is that in order to understand the problems, or better, to devise solutions, we need to start with the whole frog, in this case with education's ecosystem.

EDUCATION'S ENTANGLED BANK

Darwin asks us "to contemplate an entangled bank," with "elaborately constructed forms . . . dependent on each other in so complex a manner," which have "been produced by laws acting around us." He recognized that natural selection based on random variation led to differential reproductive fitness. The drive to adapt and reproduce in complex, changing circumstances leads to the evolution of "endless forms most beautiful and most wonderful." There is "grandeur in this view of life."[2]

Within education there is a similar entangled bank, with endless forms for learning. These support an infinite variety of topics, a variety of aims, different learning styles and histories, and different material circumstances. A law for learners corresponding to natural selection is the drive to make sense of experience, as Dewey says, to extract at each present time the full meaning of each present experience. Making meaning in that way, whether in formal or informal settings, is what prepares us for future life, which is above all to continue that sense-making. This is why interpretation may be the most important of the five ecosystem characteristics.

From simple beginnings, both biologic and learning ecosystems develop complexity in both organisms (learners) and niches. There is no simple algorithm for navigating these systems, but there is "grandeur" in their variety and complexity.

The examples in this book purposefully range across a wide diversity of learning experiences, including various ages of learners, formal and informal settings, knowledge-focused and action- or community-focused approaches, nations, and time periods. The ecosystems perspective addresses this diversity, and the divides we see represented in the scope of journals and conferences, curriculum materials, and pedagogical theories.

The perspective of *education's ecosystem* sees *diversity in modes of learning* in an expansive way. But it also examines *interaction among these types of learning, emergence, finding and constructing learning niches*, and *interpretation of learning spaces*. These elements are always present for learning, but we can work toward making them more holistic, engaging, and relevant. An educational ecosystems understanding is thus simply a tool, which helps us see how education is working and how it falls short, but it can also be employed to show us what can be done to improve it.

A PESSIMISTIC NOTE

Education can be enriched and made more relevant by connecting across formal and informal learning, school and daily life, action and reflection. The examples here show that engaging in meaningful work to build better communities can help the individual develop as well. Many of these examples (and numerous others not included) are inspiring. But despite their promise, the same examples are often successes in the near term but failures in the long.

The sad reality in many instances is that their ecosystems awareness does not extend to aligning with the most powerful forces in education's ecosystems. Among these, three stand out. First is the pressure to prepare workers with specific technical skills, who are conveniently presorted by ability level to serve the needs of global capitalism. Second is the desire of governments for, as Baldwin writes, "a citizenry which will simply obey the rules."[3] Third is the unwillingness of a public to support equitable education for all, which values diversity, citizenship, and full human development.

In contrast, the education we do have survives by aligning itself with those three powerful forces. It has less concern for aligning itself with other aspects of the ecosystem, such as family, play, arts and music, nature, or community projects, much less with critical analysis and challenges to the established order.

This gloomy note highlights an important aspect of the relation between education and democracy. We often say that an educated populace is important to build and maintain democracy. It is less often said that democracy is essential for holistic education. If the governing powers are content with, or even prefer, one kind of education for the wealthy and one for the poor, then it is not possible to have truly progressive education. If the primary criterion for success is performance on narrowly defined skills or retrieval of small bits of knowledge, then education cannot fully support the development of critical thinking or integrative learning.

CREATING DEMOCRACY

Education that values social justice, natural environments, and democratic access is an oxymoron when limited to the already privileged. Dewey's challenge is even more pertinent today: "What the best and wisest parent wants for his own child, that must the community want for all of its children. Any other ideal for our schools is narrow and unlovely; acted upon, it destroys our democracy."[4]

Pervasive inequity in education across nations, social class, race, gender, language, and other social dimensions brings up difficult questions: Why are children of the wealthy the most likely to partake of experiential education and open classrooms, whereas the children of the poor are left to wonder whether they can have any schooling at all?[5] How often do progressive educators nurture democracy within their own classrooms but remain insulated from these inequities? Do methods labeled progressive meet the needs of marginalized students, or do they merely reinforce existing power relations?[6]

A diverse and inclusive community of learning is key to both social and intellectual flourishing. Schools should become sites for democratic living, supporting community life and freedom for individuals to grow in ways that meet their needs. This is not only an end goal for schooling, but a means, the daily enactment of what democracy can be and how it can work.

At Hull-House, Jane Addams saw that "much of the insensibility and hardness of the world is due to the lack of imagination which prevents a realization of the experiences of other people."[7] She went further to argue that inclusiveness is not simply about fairness.

Inclusive education is a necessary process for bringing new ideas and divergent perspectives into inquiry. And it is vital for moral development. Addams sought what she calls *social ethics*. This extends beyond the classical view of ethics as a set of virtues that an upright individual might attain, such as tolerance, honesty, courage, or loyalty. Instead, it recognizes the essential networked nature of social life, and asks us to consider the larger context for ethical life.

The robber baron of her day might be honest in the sense that he would not cheat at cards with his friends. This might qualify him as ethical in a classical sense. But if his employment practices resulted in misery for his workers, he would score poorly on social ethics. Addams recognized that this meant that learning, ethical behavior, and ultimately democratic life depended upon meaningful social interaction with all sorts of people. If we

> consciously limit our intercourse to certain kinds of people whom we have previously decided to respect, we not only tremendously circumscribe our range of life, but limit the scope of our ethics. . . . Thus, the identification with the common lot which is the essential idea of Democracy becomes the source and expression of social ethics.[8]

When asked to write for his own second Festschrift, Dewey chose the topic of democracy. Instead of portraying it as an alternative to other forms of government, such as monarchy, theocracy, or feudal hierarchy, he argues that democracy is the idea of community life itself. Furthermore, it is not a fixed structure that can be imposed on others, but a process to be continually recreated by citizens. *Creative democracy* is the belief that lived experience generates both the goals and means for enhancing future experiences.[9] Kenneth Westhues describes this as a process of change: "Freedom is not so much a condition people live in as a process they enact, with every new assault they make on the way things are."[10]

This definition rejects the idea of democracy as a fixed mode of sociopolitical organization; instead it is to collaboratively create freer and more humane experience, based on faith in our shared experiences and learning. Democracy in this view is an active process, one that both enacts and creates meaning.[11]

Schools are not instruments for predefined social change. But as seedbeds of enriched experiences, they establish conditions for people to engage in living together without violence and working toward shared goals. Thus, experience, education, participation, colloquium, a robust public sphere, democracy, and ongoing transformation are inextricably linked. Benjamin Barber defines this as *strong democracy*, meaning broad participation of constituents in the direction and operation of political systems (the process of authority), rather than simply responding to government initiatives or being represented distantly by others.[12]

How do our political institutions, industrial arrangements, or, for that matter, universities fare in terms of contributing to "the all-around growth of every member of society"?[13] Rather than fostering growth, many ignore the issue; they operate as if purely technical procedures tell us all we need to know about life, community, and moral commitment. There are alternative models of how institutions can promote individual growth, which provide us with a more sustainable and ecologically sound vision for flourishing communities and individuals, but even bringing those models into mainstream discourse is a daunting challenge.

It is clear that the future of democracy and of democratic education are mutually constituted. Accordingly, the discussion cannot remain shackled to high-stakes, low-rationale testing, nor can we accept the continual degradation of the public education ideal, even if it has rarely been fully achieved in practice. Above all, we need healthy dialogue about what we want our schools and communities to be, and ultimately, what we want ourselves to be. Writing at the end of his new compilation of case studies on American democracy, David Moss says that the "essence of democratic governance . . . always comes back to the people, their conception of how collective decisions ought to be made, and to what end. This is why ongoing debate about the democracy itself—both past and present—has historically been such a vital part of American life."[14]

THE CAPACITY FOR LIFE

In his autobiography, Pablo Casals offers one model revealing his love of the natural world: "I do not think a day passes in my life in which I fail to look with fresh amazement at the miracle of nature. It is there on every side. It can be simply a shadow on a mountainside, or a spider's web gleaming with dew, or sunlight on the leaves of a tree."[15] He continues with a lament about education failing to measure up to both the beauty of life and its challenges:

> Sometimes I look about me with a feeling of complete dismay. In the confusion that afflicts the world today, I see a disrespect for the very values of life. . . . Each second we live in a new and unique moment of the universe, a moment that never was before and will never be again. And what do we teach our children in school? We teach them that two and two make four, and that Paris is the capital of France. When will we also teach them what they are?

If we believe that education must be more than the instillation of inert ideas, what then should we do? Casals recognizes that learning about the universe is first of all learning about one's self:

> We should say to them: Do you know what you are? You are a marvel. You are unique. In all of the world there is no other child exactly like you. In the millions of years that have passed there has never been another child like you. And look at your body—what a wonder it is! Your legs, your arms, your cunning fingers, the way you move! . . . You have the capacity of anything. And when you grow up, can you then harm another who is, like you, a marvel? You must cherish one another. You must work—we all must work—to make this world worthy of its children.[16]

NOTES

1. Cesar Chavez, *Education of the Heart: Cesar Chavez in His Own Words* (Los Angeles, CA: The Cesar E. Chavez Foundation, 1995), para. 16.
2. Charles Darwin, *On the Origin of Species by Means of Natural Selection* (London: John Murray, Albermarle Street, 1859), 490.
3. James Baldwin, "A Talk to Teachers," *The Saturday Review*, December 21, 1963, 42.
4. John Dewey, *The School and Society*, MW 1:5.
5. James D. Anderson, *The Education of Blacks in the South, 1860–1935* (Chapel Hill: University of North Carolina Press, 1988); Samuel Bowles and Herbert Gintis, *Schooling in Capitalist America: Educational Reform and the Contradictions of Economic Life* (Chicago: Haymarket Books, 2014); Ida B. Wells, *Crusade for Justice: The Autobiography of Ida B. Wells* (Chicago: University of Chicago Press, 1972).
6. Lisa D. Delpit, *"Multiplication Is for White People": Raising Expectations for Other People's Children* (New York: New Press, 2012).
7. Jane Addams, *Democracy and Social Ethics* (Chicago: University of Illinois Press, 2002, original work published in 1902), 8.
8. Jane Addams, *Democracy and Social Ethics* (Urbana, IL: University of Illinois Press, 2002), 8–9.
9. John Dewey, "Creative Democracy: The Task before Us," LW 14:229, 229–30.
10. Kenneth Westhues, *First Sociology* (New York: McGraw-Hill, 1982), 444.
11. Hans Joas, *The Creativity of Action* (Chicago: University of Chicago Press, 1996).
12. Benjamin R. Barber, *Strong Democracy: Participatory Politics for a New Age* (Berkeley, CA: University of California Press, 2003).
13. John Dewey, "Reconstruction in Philosophy," MW 12:8–201.
14. David A. Moss, *Democracy: A Case Study* (Cambridge, MA: Harvard University Press, 2017), 694.
15. Pablo Casals, *Joys & Sorrows* (London: Eel Pie Publishing, 1981), 17.
16. Ibid., 295.

Bibliographic Note

References to John Dewey's writing are to *The Collected Works of John Dewey, 1882–1953*, edited by Jo Ann Boydston (Carbondale and Edwardsville: Southern Illinois University Press, 1969–1991). SIU Press publishes this in three series: *The Early Works* (EW), *The Middle Works* (MW), and *The Later Works* (LW). For example, LW 13:29 refers to *The Later Works*, volume 13, page 29.

Index

activity center, 87
Adams, Henry, 103–104
Addams, Jane, 36, 51, 63, 88, 148, 155–156
apprenticeship, xiii
assessment, 117, 119, 144

banking model, 102, 119, 120, 127, 133, 136, 140
Bauhaus, 108, 110–112, 113, 114n6, 115n18, 115n20
biodiversity, 4, 5, 14, 16, 20, 21, 41, 53, 101, 146, 154
Black Mountain College, 108–110, 113–114

Camara, 73–74, 80
Casals, Pablo, 157–158
CeRe. *See* Resource Centre for Public Participation
Chickscope, 74, 77, 78–80
citizen, socially engaged, xiii, xx, xxiii, 9, 24–25, 30, 31, 33, 34, 71, 89, 91, 93, 94–95, 97, 101, 106, 123, 124, 145, 150, 156
cognition, 51–53; embedded, xix, 46, 50, 51, 52–53, 54; embodied, 46, 47, 49, 50, 51–52; extended, 46, 51–54
cognitive science, 51
community: as intellectual space, 61, 87, 89; engagement, xix, 8, 32, 35, 50, 51, 72, 89, 94, 95, 125, 133; health, xxvii, 19, 26, 28, 35, 51, 60, 61, 80, 86, 87, 89, 132, 144, 145, 146
community-based, 57, 149; education, 86, 89, 94; research, 64n7, 64n13
construction of learning niches, 6
critical pedagogy, 36, 61, 132, 145

dance, 43, 50, 52, 85, 125
Darwin, Charles, 13, 17, 19, 42, 153
Davies, Joseph Ilott, 13–18, 21n4, 21n10, 25
democracy, xxiii, xxiv, 1, 13, 24, 30, 33–35, 60, 71, 88, 99n17, 107, 111, 138, 148, 155, 156–157; as a way of life, 108
development, moral, xx, 3, 27, 29, 31, 70, 110, 117, 135, 156
Dewey, John, 32–33, 36, 52, 72, 75, 81, 88, 110, 113, 150, 154, 155, 156
diversity of learning, 4, 42–55

Easley, Jack, 121, 122, 128n7, 147
ecological: invalidity, 6, 7; niche, 3, 4, 5, 16, 18, 20, 45, 83–84, 95, 133
ecopedagogy, 144–145
ecosystem: awareness, 58–59, 61, 142, 150, 154; biological, xiv–xv, 3, 4, 11n6, 16–17, 19–21, 37, 54, 83, 145
Ecosystems Learning Framework (ELF), xiii, xxiii, xxvii–xxviii, 2–10, 20, 63.

See also diversity of learning, networking, emergence, construction of learning niches, interpretation of learning niches
education: democratic, xxiii–xxiv, 23–24, 33–35, 62, 63, 72, 89, 91, 95, 106, 120, 132, 138, 145, 148, 150, 155–157; quality of, xxv, 119, 124. *See also* learning
educational: biography, 103–104; web, 95
emergence, xxi, 58, 67, 101, 146, 154; emergent property, xiii, xix, xxv, xxviii, 4, 5–6, 20, 67–81, 147–148
Escuela Nueva, 72, 89–90
evaluation: school, 35, 137; student; teacher, 35, 136

Freinet, Célestin, 70–73, 74, 127, 150
frog, xxvii, 14–18

Gropius, Ati, 104–114, 114n8
Gropius, Walter, 108, 110, 111

hooks, bell, 1, 150
Hull-House, 63, 155

Illich, Ivan, 95, 120, 134
inequity, 155
intelligence: civic, 34, 98, 150; socially engaged, xxiii, 135. *See also* socially engaged citizen
interpretation of learning niches, 6, 7, 8, 101–114, 149, 154

Kropotkin, Peter, 19, 22n14

learning: bahal, 45–49, 49, 51, 93, 98, 103, 143; community-based. *See* community; ecosystem; ecosystems learning framework; experiential, xiii–xiv, xx, xxviii, 50, 75, 89, 104, 155; integrated, 3, 49, 54, 74, 80, 85, 97, 135, 147, 150; lifelong, xix, 27, 31, 42, 84, 113, 114, 117, 122, 134; niche; diversity of learning; walks, 71, 127
Libanius, 134–135
lichen, 19, 57, 67, 68, 69, 84
life, everyday, 7, 53, 87, 97, 120, 124, 126, 127, 133–134, 140, 145, 148

magnetic resonance imaging (MRI), 74, 75, 76, 77, 78, 79, 80
media: digital, 9, 95–96, 98; new, xx, xxiv, xxviii, 9, 74, 77, 80, 96–98, 117, 142, 147; social, xxiv, 3, 27, 50, 84, 96, 97, 137, 142. *See also* information and communication technology
Misiones Pedagógicas, 91–93, 99n17
Museum School, Fort Worth, xvii–xx
music, 44, 51, 92, 98, 125, 144

Nazi Germany, 104, 105, 106

open educational resources (OER), 96

participatory action research, 97
Paseo Boricua, 57–63
Pedro Albizu Campos High School (PACHS), 57–62
Peirce, Charles Sanders, 69, 84, 122
PLATO, 95–96
Plutarch, 101, 102, 134
Popular Education (*La Educación popular*), 62, 72
poverty, xxv, 35
privatization, 120, 126
problem solving, 46, 74, 122, 124, 140
progressive education, 34–35, 35–36, 86–89, 95, 135; network, xiii

racism, xxiv, 8, 25, 27, 58, 60, 63, 124, 142
reasoning, 69, 106, 113, 124, 130
Resource Centre for Public Participation (CeRe), 94–95
Russell, Bertrand, 13, 106, 113
Russell, Dora, 106, 120

service learning, 61, 89
sexism, 63, 142
social: center, xiv, 2, 9, 60, 88, 97; ecology, 61, 142; emotional learning, 10, 45, 47, 48, 61
State of Wellfleet Harbor Conference, 84–85

technology: information and communication, 2, 51, 53, 73, 80, 96, 97–98, 147 urban agriculture, 61, 63, 64n13

visual art, 93, 125

Whitehead, Alfred North, 51, 55, 81, 123
Wikipedia, 73, 96, 142

Youth Community Inquiry (YCI), 97

About the Author

Bertram Bruce has a PhD in computer science and is currently a professor emeritus in information science at the University of Illinois. He has worked on education in many countries, across grade levels, and in diverse areas of the curriculum. His work contributes to a tradition of democratic education, asking, "How can we guide the educational enterprise by an ethical vision, not simply a technocratic one of transmitting isolated facts and skills?"

www.ingramcontent.com/pod-product-compliance
Lightning Source LLC
Chambersburg PA
CBHW051811230426
43672CB00012B/2698